The Multidimensional Pastor

The Multidimensional Pastor

The Many Facets of Pastoral Ministry

SAMSON L. UYTANLET

RESOURCE *Publications* · Eugene, Oregon

THE MULTIDIMENSIONAL PASTOR
The Many Facets of Pastoral Ministry

Copyright © 2020 Samson L. Uytanlet. All rights reserved. Except for brief quotations in critical publications or reviews, no part of this book may be reproduced in any manner without prior written permission from the publisher. Write: Permissions, Wipf and Stock Publishers, 199 W. 8th Ave., Suite 3, Eugene, OR 97401.

Illustration by: Jansen Lee

Unless otherwise indicated, Scripture quotations are from the ESV® Bible (The Holy Bible, English Standard Version®), copyright © 2001 by Crossway Bibles, a publishing ministry of Good News Publishers. Used by permission. All rights reserved.

Resource Publications
An Imprint of Wipf and Stock Publishers
199 W. 8th Ave., Suite 3
Eugene, OR 97401

www.wipfandstock.com

PAPERBACK ISBN: 978-1-7252-7292-7
HARDCOVER ISBN: 978-1-7252-7291-0
EBOOK ISBN: 978-1-7252-7293-4

Manufactured in the U.S.A.   06/16/20

In memory of
Susana Uytanlet Garcia (1954–2019)
Olivia Uytanlet (1962–2020)

Do you love me? Shepherd my sheep!

—Jesus

Contents

Preface		ix
Acknowledgments		xi
Abbreviations		xiii
The Pastor as a Superhuman?		1
1	The Pastor as a Human	4
2	The Pastor as a Servant	16
3	The Pastor as a Counselor	29
4	The Pastor as a Disciple-Maker	41
5	The Pastor as a Teacher/Trainer	53
6	The Pastor as an Exegete/Prophet	65
7	The Pastor as an Evangelist/Apologist	77
8	The Pastor as a Theologian/Ethicist	88
9	The Pastor as a Manager	99
10	The Pastor as a Family Person	110
11	The Pastor as a Liturgist	120
12	The Pastor as a Hermit	131
The Pastor is Not a Superhuman!		142
Bibliography		145
Author Index		149
Subject Index		151
Scripture Index		155

Preface

WHAT IS A PASTOR? What are their responsibilities? The answer to these two questions may vary from one denomination to another, from church to church, even from individual to individual. We all have our expectations from pastors—how they carry themselves and what they wear, how they talk and behave, what work they do, and many more. Whether we are aware of it, our expectations from a pastor reflects our theological understanding of the pastoral ministry.

For some, a pastor is someone who does house visitations two to three times a week, leads the prayer meeting every Wednesday, and preaches every Sunday. Only those who fulfill these requirements are pastors. For others, the primary role of the pastor is preaching on Sundays, leading Bible studies, and teaching Sunday school. As long as the pastor can feed the congregation spiritually, they have done their job. There are also those who see their pastor as the church administrator, punches the time card daily at 8 a.m. and 5 p.m., ready to take phone calls 24/7, and makes sure the "operation" of the church is smooth. There are also those who think that pastors should not be inside the church office, but they should be going out "where the people are" and sharing the Gospel to them.

Each of these views has some merit, but they all focus only on one area of the pastor's ministry while overlooking other important ones. In this work, my aim is to broaden our understanding of the roles of the pastors, yet at the same time, develop a more realistic expectation from a pastor. As we understand the roles of the pastors better, pastors can explore other areas of ministry in which they can be involved; and as we learn to see our personal limitations in doing ministry, we can learn to appreciate the work of fellow pastors knowing that they are our coworkers.

Acknowledgments

A NUMBER OF PASTORS and seminary professors have influenced the way I understand the pastor's ministry. Many of the things I wrote in this book, I have learned from them. It seems fitting that I mention them as an acknowledgement of their work. Rev. David Moldez is one of the pastors who consistently exemplifies humility and a heart of a servant. He was the academic dean of Central Bible Seminary (CBS) during my first couple of years as a student and he became the president before I finished my undergraduate studies in Theology. His Christlike character is one of the things that inspire me as I enter the ministry. Many of my teachers at CBS deserves acknowledgement as well. From Rev. Antonio Hermano, I learned the importance of doing contextual theology. Rev. Jaime Tabingo showed us the importance of understanding the various religious groups as we prepare to answer questions about Christianity. Dr. Hermann Moldez was my first Homiletics teacher, and he taught us the importance of loving the Scripture to be effective in preaching. Ptr. John Tayoto gave us a lot of practical advice on church administration.

As an MDiv student at the Alliance Graduate School, there are also professors from whom I learned about the pastoral ministry. Dr. Rodrigo Tano was another teacher who reminded us of the importance of contextual theology and exemplified how it can be done. Bishop Valmike Apuzen was my Pastoral Ministry teacher, and as the head of the Christian and Missionary Alliance Churches of the Philippines (CAMACOP) at that time, he was able to share to us real examples of what to expect in the ministry, how to troubleshoot problems, and what can be done to prevent problems in the church.

Three of my colleagues at the Biblical Seminary of the Philippines are also worth mentioning here. Rev. Wilson Gokiao, who retired a few years ago, is an example of gentleness. His genuine desire to train a successor before his retirement, and the method he used is one that I can always look back to as a model. Dr. David Chang modeled simplicity and diligence, not only to the students, but also to the professors. No one in the seminary can miss out the pastor's heart of Rev. Philip Co, who genuinely cares for both our students and our coworkers in the seminary.

Abbreviations

CGJ	*Common Ground Journal*
ChrCent	*Christian Century*
ClerJ	*Clergy Journal*
CTR	*Criswell Theological Review*
Enc	*Encounter*
FT	*First Things*
HvTSt	*Hervormde Teologiese Studies*
JBCoun	*Journal for Biblical Counseling*
PPsy	*Pastoral Psychology*
Prism	*Prism*
Touch	*Touchstone*
Vision	*Vision*
Worship	*Worship*

The Pastor as a Superhuman?

YEARS AGO, I ATTENDED a pastor's conference where I met pastors from other churches. Some of them I already knew, others I have met for the first time. One pastor gave me his business card indicating his position in the church that reads, "Senior Pastor and CEO." That was the first time I saw a pastor being referred to as CEO and my initial thought was, "Has the church become a business?" Admittedly, there are some similarities between the responsibilities of a senior pastor and those of a CEO of a company; but of course, there are still more differences. My purpose for sharing this encounter is not to evaluate whether it is correct to use the title CEO for senior pastors, but to illustrate that our view of the pastoral ministry is constantly evolving. In fact, pastoral ministry is also changing through time.

The changing times, the needs of the congregation and the larger community, and the various contexts where we minister are just few of the factors that require flexibility in the way we do pastoral ministry. Our approach to the ministry may develop, but the core values and principles of pastoral ministry need not change. The reason is because the principles from the Scripture is unchanging even if its expressions may require modifications. My purpose in writing this work is to identify the various roles of the pastors and to lay out scriptural principles related to these various aspects of the pastoral ministry. The way the pastors fulfill these roles may vary, but the essential principles for pastoral ministry remain the same.

The starting point of our discussion concerning the pastoral ministry is the pastor's shared humanity with the rest of the world. Being a pastor does not make one less or more human. It is true that the Jesus taught his followers to be different, to be in the world but not of the world (John 17:14–17), to not conform to the patterns of the world (Rom 12:1), but this principle of non-conformity applies in situations when the patterns of the world are against God and his ways. Each of us should be able to identify cultural ideals and practices that, although not taught in the Scripture, are not contrary to the principles of the Bible. Even as followers of Christ, we should be able to point out some social expectations, values, and standards that, even though are not Christian in origin, but are consistent with the teachings of the Scripture. There are some social and cultural values and ideals that we need not abandon just because we are followers of Jesus. Keeping in mind that the God Incarnate allowed himself to be bound by Jewish cultural norms and practices, while boldly speaking against those that defy God's standards.

Being a pastor is more than just being human who can relate with their world. At the core of the identity of pastors is a servant. This is what Jesus exemplified while he shepherded his flock, and this is what he expects from those who wanted to be shepherds of his people. The other roles of the pastors must spring out of their core identity as a servant, as Figure 1 shows. We may consider the expression "servant leadership" a cliché; but it is what leadership is supposed to be. It has become a cliché only because it is a correct principle often taught, but seldom practiced. It is up to us to not let this overused expression lose its real meaning.

In this work, I will discuss ten various roles of pastors that spring out of their shared humanity with their flock and their identity as servant. These roles are: counselor, disciple-maker, teacher/trainer, exegete/prophet, evangelist/apologist, theologian/ethicist, manager, family person, liturgist, and hermit.

The task of pastoral care begins with a pastoral heart, which requires an attitude of a servant. The heart of a pastor as *counselor* must be like a public square where anyone can freely come regardless of gender, personality, social status, race, religion, political views, educational attainment, or nature of work.

It is the pastor's servant-attitude as a *disciple-maker* that can make them see people, not for who they are at present, but for who they can be as God transforms their life. This vision should motivate them to invest their life and time on others so they can also become disciples of Jesus.

The same attitude is required of the *teacher/trainer* because it reminds them of their own limitations and see the contributions that other members of the body of Christ can give for the building up of the body. This is the attitude that enables a pastor to rejoice as they see how God uses others to glorify him.

Serving others should be the primary motivation of the pastor as an *exegete/prophet*. Interpreting and speaking God's word is not to be done for self-aggrandizement, but as a way to lead God's people in understanding his message for them.

The same mindset must be with the pastors who do the work of an *evangelist/apologist*. Although persuading a person to believe and follow Jesus is essentially the work of the Spirit, the evangelist's attitude as they present the gospel message can potentially turn hearers away and make them reject the message.

Pastors who assume the role of a *theologian/ethicist* must also have a servant's heart. Doing theological reflections and defining ethical standards can easily be done with an "I-am-better-than-them" attitude. Only theologians with a servant's heart can be clear with God's standards while appreciating the extent of his redemption.

As pastors assume the role of a *manager*, they must continue to exhibit Christ's attitude of humility. As managers, the pastors must remember that their coworkers are not tools that they can utilize, but fellow servants who serve the same Master with them.

Pastors are not only to manage the church; they ought to manage their family as well. As a *family person*, pastors must make sure that they do not neglect their own family because the members of their family are also members of their flock who are related to them; thus, they must serve them as well.

As leader of the congregation, the pastor does not only manage the household of God, but they also lead them in worship. As a *liturgist*, the pastor leads the congregation in serving God in ways that please, honor, and glorify him.

The servants of God need time alone with their Master, like a *hermit* who spends extended time with God. These are necessary breaks in the pastor's ministry, not only to rest and be refreshed, but also to have time to reflect on God's direction for their work, to renew their commitment to serve, and to regain strength for the work ahead.

These are the various roles of the pastor we will be discussing in the next ten chapters.

Figure 1: The Many Facets of Pastoral Ministry

The work of the pastors emanates from the fact that they are humans called by God to serve both him and his people.

1

The Pastor as a Human

Persons called to the clergy profession live always in the tension between two realities: their humanity—who and what they are, their best and their worst, their gifts and their limits—and the special demands of their calling.[1]

—WALTER E. WIEST AND ELWYN A. SMITH

BEFORE WE CAN THINK about becoming a pastor, we must first reflect on what it means to be human. At times, pastors are not effective in ministry, not because they lack the gifts and talents to do the work, but because they lack the rudimentary social skills like courtesy or politeness. At other times, pastors are not able to present the teachings of the Scripture, not because they lack oratorical skills or theological knowledge, but because they are insensitive to the cultural norms of the people to whom they communicate.

The incarnation of Jesus is the basic premise in saying that the pastoral ministry begins by being human. God had always been a shepherd of his people, but the Word still became flesh to minister to his flock. Jesus was born a Jew; he had an ethnicity like the rest of humanity. He needed the care of his human parents, like every human does. He had parents that brought

---

1. Wiest and Smith, *Ethics in Ministry*, 97.

him up according to the ways of Judaism; he was born with a religion, attending religious festivals in the temple and synagogue meetings. He was a son of a carpenter; and had likely learned the same trade. He interacted socially with people, attended weddings and other social gatherings. He built friendships with some people, and wept for his friend at his funeral. He paid taxes to Caesar, and taught others to do the same. In his interactions with people, he expressed various emotions like grief, anger, compassion, and joy. In short, he became human to serve humans.

Jesus allowed himself to be subjected to the social, cultural, political, and religious limitations of being human. He ministered to his flock by sharing their humanity. As ministers who wanted to follow the footsteps of the Master, we must remember that the starting point of pastoral ministry is acknowledging our shared humanity with the rest of the world. Thus, before thinking about being a pastor, we must first make sure we are being HUMAN: it starts by being Humane, by being aware of how our Upbringing shaped us, by developing proper Manners, by having the right Attitude, and by understanding our Nature.

START BY BEING HUMAN

Humane

The parable of the good Samaritan is one of the well-known stories Jesus had told. The story was a response to the question of a lawyer who, after being reminded by Jesus to love his neighbor, asked, "Who is my neighbor?" Jesus told about a priest and a Levite who did not show compassion to a person who fell victim to a robber. Instead, it was a Samaritan who took the extra mile to help the assaulted traveler, "But a Samaritan, as he journeyed, came to where he was, and when he saw him, *he had compassion*" (Luke 10:33, italics added). The victim was going to Jerusalem from Jericho. Jerusalem was the center of Judaism; this may suggest that the victim was a Jew. He was ignored by the Jewish religious leaders but was unexpectedly shown compassion by a Samaritan. Human compassion is the expression of love for neighbors. On the one hand, this story is a slap on the face of the "honorable religious leaders" who could not show the same compassion to their neighbor. On the other hand, it reflects the reality that compassion is a basic human virtue that even the "despicable Samaritan" knew that it was right.

One does not need to be a believer of Jesus to have the capacity to show mercy and compassion. Human's ability to be compassionate toward others is evidence that every person, despite our sinfulness, still bear the image of the compassionate God who had repeatedly shown compassion even toward an undeserving and rebellious people. Even in disciplining his people, God remained compassionate toward them (2 Kgs 13:23). By sending the prophets to warn his people of possible judgment, God shows his compassion to his people (2 Chr 36:15). Those who claim to be believers of God must all the more exhibit this quality because it reflects the quality of the God they serve. Michael R. Emlet points to God as our prime example of compassion:

> As saints, we need confirmation of our identity in Christ; as sufferers, we need comfort in the midst of affliction; and as sinners, we need challenge to our sin in light of God's redemptive mercies to us in Jesus Christ. If God shepherds his people in these ways, then the same broad biblical categories should also guide the shape of our love as ministers to those around us in both formal and informal settings.[2]

God commanded the Israelites to show compassion by not taking another person's cloak as an overnight pledge for the latter's debt, and the reason is because he is the compassionate God (Exod 22:26–27). We cannot assume that the quality of human compassion toward fellow humans can match that of God. Even in showing mercy, we may be driven by selfish motives. Nonetheless, we cannot deny the fact that humans have the ability to be compassionate.

Humans do not only have the ability to be compassionate; they also have the ability to be cruel. Cruelty and the lack of compassion are generally deemed as undesirable traits. Hence, we proclaim the message of life transformation that Jesus offers. Christianity is not the only religion that teaches compassion. Being compassionate is part of being sensible humans. The so-called Golden Rule, for instance, was taught not only by Jesus and Confucius, but also by many ancient sages. Although they expressed the rule of reciprocity differently, the various versions are essentially the same. This Golden Rule of reciprocity encompasses all virtues, including compassion. The one who expects compassion must be willing to show compassion. As imitators of Jesus, it is one of his character that pastors must all the more strive to have.

Becoming a pastor begins by being human, and this requires us to acknowledge the depravity, the weaknesses, and the need we share with the rest of humanity. As we learn to see others as humans who, just like us, need compassion at different points in their life, we can learn how to show mercy even toward those who wronged us, kindness toward those who are in need, and compassion to those who are in pain.

---

2. Emlet, "Loving Others as Saints, Sufferer, and Sinners," 40.

Upbringing

Our upbringing inevitably affects our personality and character; and consequently, the way we do ministry. Reggie McNeal suggests six areas of the leader's life that shape them: (1) culture—the historical and socio-political environments which include both positive and negative forces; (2) call—the leader's personal conviction about the unique mission God has for them; (3) community—the leader's family of origin and friendships; (4) communion—the leader's conscious cultivation of his relationship with God; (5) conflict—various challenges encountered; and (6) commonplace—day to day encounters of the leader.[3] The third one, in particular, is most relevant to our discussion here.

Pastors must be aware of the social and cultural environment that molded them causing them to see things, relate with others, make decisions, and respond to particular situations in a certain way. McNeal further notes that the leader's family of origin is one of the biggest factors for their vulnerabilities, and that the "difference between healthy and unhealthy leaders often rests on the leader's willingness or unwillingness to explore these early heart lessons. Doing so yields insights that can free the leader through self-understanding. Failure to do so keeps the leader chained to the past and tormented by mysterious forces that are not understood."[4]

Ronald D. Sisk identifies three reasons we do not often discuss the effects of the pastor's upbringing on his ministry: (1) the Christian faith is about new beginnings, thus our past is often overlooked; (2) we often discount the power of the past; and (3) seminary curricula often focus on the academic contents.[5]

A few examples from the Scripture illustrates that a minister's upbringing helped shape them, inevitably affecting their work, whether positively or negatively. Paul, for instance, described his upbringing this way, "circumcised on the eighth day, of the people of Israel, of the tribe of Benjamin, a Hebrew of Hebrews; as to the law, a Pharisee; as to zeal, a persecutor of the church; as to righteousness under the law, blameless" (Phil 3:5–6). Paul's circumcision on the eighth day says more about his parents than about him. It shows that they were conscientious Jews who were careful to follow the requirements of the Law of Moses (Lev 12:3). Clearly, no eight-day-old baby can bring himself to the priest for circumcision. Someone must bring them to the priest, and it is usually the parents (see also Luke 1:59; 2:21). With

---

3. McNeal, *A Work of Heart*, xxii–xxiii.
4. McNeal, *A Work of Heart*, 117–18.
5. Sisk, *The Competent Pastor*, 5–7.

pious parents, it is not surprising that Paul grew up to be a zealous Jew despite living in the Diaspora.

Paul's training to be a Pharisee can also be partially credited to his parents because his education can only be possible with the support of his family members. The strict religious environment within which Paul grew explains his zeal that made him a persecutor of the Christians. In the same way, Peter's religious background made him refuse God's invitation to eat unclean animals (Acts 11:5–10); and it also affected the way he related with Gentiles. God had to do something drastic to change Peter's perception about the "unclean" Gentiles.

In the case of Moses, he grew up in an environment where there was hostility between the host people (the Egyptians) and their slaves (the Hebrews). He lived among the royal family of Egypt, but he knew that he was one of the Hebrew slaves. His situation was not ideal. No wonder when he saw an Egyptian beating a Hebrew slave, Moses came to the rescue by killing the Egyptian (Exod 2:11–12). Hostile environment can make people hostile, even if it is only for self-preservation.

The lives of Moses and Paul, on the one hand, show how one's upbringing affects who we are as a person, the things we deem important, and our passions. On the other hand, their lives also show that *transformation is possible*. Christ's offer of hope should not blind us to the power of our past, neither should the influence of our upbringing keep us from seeing the power of Christ. In fact, Christ's power to transform makes most sense because of human sin, both of the pastors and of those who molded them. Our upbringing can have both positive and negative effects on us. Being aware of this can help the pastor thank God for the positive ones and trust God to transform the negative ones. This is part of being human.

Manners

There are customs unique for a particular culture, and there are those that go beyond the cultural divide. Some practices may be acceptable in one culture but offensive in another. There are practices that are inconsistent with the teachings of the Scripture, and in cases like this, the Christian's best choice is to obey the Scripture even if it may appear offensive. However, there are practices that are not morally wrong according to the Scripture's standards, and the correct thing to do is to be sensitive, to understand, and to follow the local manners and customs.

Whether a person is a local, a migrant, or a transient, one of the basic forms of courtesy is understanding the local manners and customs so that we do not unnecessarily offend anyone by our misbehaviors. Every person must be aware of these cultural practices, and pastors are not exempt from this requirement.

There are customs that may be unique to a particular culture. For example, there were marriage practices that are not practiced universally. Jacob was cheated and was forced to marry Leah even after Laban agreed to give him Rachel. Laban clearly deceived Jacob, but when confronted by Jacob, he made an excuse, "It is not so done in our country, to give the younger before the firstborn" (Gen 29:26).[6] Another custom that is not practiced universally is greeting someone or bidding another farewell with kisses. We see numerous examples of this both in the Old and New Testaments.

There are also customs that are shared by many cultures. For instance, courtesy and gratitude is something commendable in most countries. Of course, their expressions may differ, but their basic purpose is similar. No wonder after Jesus healed the ten lepers, the failure of the nine to show gratitude is considered inappropriate. Hence, Jesus asked, "Were not ten cleansed? Where are the nine? Was no one found to return and give praise to God except this foreigner?" (Luke 17:17–18). For Jesus, ungratefulness is synonymous with evil, "But love your enemies, and do good, and lend, expecting nothing in return, and your reward will be great, and you will be sons of the Most High, for he is kind to the *ungrateful* and the *evil*" (6:35, italics added; cf. 2 Tim 3:2; Heb 12:28). Knowing how to say "thank you," "sorry," "please," and "excuse me" may sound simple, and these are lessons we normally teach children; but adults, and more so pastors, must know these social norms and basic human courtesy. Knowing how to properly address an elderly person, bowing to greet them, or standing up in their presence as a sign of respect are essential in some cultures. Using the appropriate words in conversations with certain people is also important.

Every culture also has a standard with regard to relating with the opposite sex. When the so-called "sinful woman" approached Jesus, used her tears to wash his feet and her hairs to dry them, the response of Simon the Pharisee was, "If this man were a prophet, he would have known who and what sort of woman this is who is touching him, for she is a sinner" (Luke 7:39). The reaction of Simon shows that the Jewish society in which Jesus lived had a standard of propriety in regard to dealing with the opposite sex. Jesus challenged the self-righteous attitude of the Pharisee, not the cultural norms concerning interactions between men and women.

---

6. Laban was clearly making an excuse for being deceptive; nonetheless, he could simply be taking advantage of a cultural norm to cheat Jacob.

Even in terms of clothing, certain manner of dressing is considered inappropriate in some cultures. We must not expect all cultures to share the same standard, but we must be aware of the local standards of propriety; and more importantly, the biblical standards of propriety. Take Aaron and his contemporaries for instance, being slaves in Egypt all their life, it is just natural for them to dress like the Egyptian slaves. A number of ancient Egyptian wall paintings show the male servants wearing only short skirt-like covering around their waist. We can assume that the Israelites also wore them when they came out of Egypt. Thus, when God appointed Aaron as priest, he commanded Moses to do two things. First, not to make altars with steps, "that your nakedness be not exposed on it" (Exod 20:26). Second, to make for Aaron long robe (28:4). The purpose is to avoid exposing parts of the body that should not be exposed and distract the worshippers.

Many other examples can be cited, but these are enough to show that there are manners and customs in every culture, and people should be aware of them. Pastors, all the more, must be aware of these practices and uphold those that are consistent with scriptural standards.

Attitude

Sports is more than just a game of skills; it is a mental competition as well. This is the reason some athletes swagger during competitions because it is a psychological tactic to overpower their opponents. Once athletes have mental control over their opponents and the latter begins to lose composure, then it is easier for the former to win. Actors sometimes do the same to display confidence, because the lack of it can turn many fans off. Although the influence of these athletes and movie stars on the ordinary people cannot be denied, and admiration of these stars cause many to think it is an attitude worth imitating, societies in general do not value smugness, impertinence, and pomposity.

The Scripture contains many stories illustrating the importance of humility, like the story of the Pharisee and the tax collector (Luke 18:9–14), among others. However, teachings about the importance of humility can also be found in many cultures and other religions. The ancient Greek storyteller Aesop had written several fables to teach about humility, such as the story of the lion and the wolf, the story of the turtle and the rabbit, and the story of the gnat and the lion. Modern Filipinos also tell the story of the sparrow and the carabao. An ancient Chinese proverb says, "Nobility is rooted in humility, and high founded on the low."[7] These are few examples to

---

7. Confucius, et al., *The Four Chinese Classics*, 78.

illustrate that humility is generally considered an important virtue, whether in ancient or modern times.

People naturally want to be with or to work with people who have good attitude. Our attitude can either build or destroy our relationship with others. No wonder many employers prefer to hire someone with average skills but a good attitude than someone with superior skills but a bad attitude. Humans are naturally uninclined to make friends with neighbors who are arrogant and disrespectful. Even in school, students normally avoid other students who are haughty and overbearing. People generally expect classmates, coworkers, and neighbors who are respectful, modest, and humble. These are virtues that are also considered honorable in the Scripture. Just imagine how a pastor with an attitude can minister effectively. The pastor's charisma can sometimes compensate for (or perhaps more accurately, "cover up") the lack in this area; and interestingly, overflowing confidence and strong charisma can even draw a large following. But the person with a good attitude remains preferable whether we talk about school or work, and more importantly, the pastorate.

More important than the society's expectation is the teaching of the Scripture. First, the Scripture teaches against arrogance. One part of the body that is often associated with pride are the eyes (2 Sam 22:28; Ps 18:27; Prov 6:17; 21:4; Isa 2:11; 5:15). Pride is often expressed by the way we look at others. Pride prevents us from "looking up" (respect) to others; instead, it leads us to "look down" (degrade) on others. Social status, ethnic or religious associations, physical features, talents and abilities, accomplishments, and sometimes even theological affiliations, can make people assume that they are better than others. Thus, they are entitled to look down on others who are perceived to be inferior. The Scripture's command is clear, "For by the grace given to me I say to everyone among you not to think of himself more highly than he ought to think, but to think with sober judgment, each according to the measure of faith that God has assigned" (Rom 12:3).

Second, the Scripture also associates pride with the heart, "Whoever has a haughty look and an arrogant heart I will not endure" (Ps 101:5b). Whatever is in our heart comes out of our mouths. Pride leads to boasting about one's accomplishments, and it makes one use condescending words to berate others. Whatever is in our heart also comes out through our actions. Pride leads to unnecessary display of possessions, and it glories in seeing others who have less.

Humans are naturally inclined to be proud, and those who enter the pastoral ministry are not exempted from this tendency. If we want to justify haughtiness, we will not lack reasons to do so. Charles H. Spurgeon is often quoted as saying, "Be not proud of race, face, place, or grace." The Scripture is clear, however, "Haughty eyes and a proud heart, the lamp of the wicked, are sin" (Prov 21:4). How one looks at oneself in relation to others and what comes out from our heart through our words and actions reflect our attitude. Character is still more important than charisma.

Nature

Personality, temperament, and disposition—these are few of the words we often associate with the inherent characteristics of a person. Humans have traits that distinguish one from another. It could be the way they do things (fast or slow, methodical or spontaneous, detailed or less elaborate) or the way they talk (loud or soft, direct or roundabout). These differences are not a matter of right versus wrong or good versus bad; but these characteristics show each individual's unique traits which inevitably affect the way one relates with people and the way one works. For pastors, these traits affect the way they do ministry.

Every person has their own personality traits. The twins of Isaac and Rebekah are perfect examples of this. Even though Esau and Jacob develop in the same womb and were born just minutes apart, aside from their physical appearance (Gen 25:25), their personalities distinguish one from the other, "When the boys grew up, Esau was a skillful hunter, a man of the field, while Jacob was a quiet man, dwelling in tents" (25:27). As a result, Isaac preferred the gallant and adventurous Esau, and Rebekah loved the homebody Jacob (25:28). Esau's love of the outdoors does not have anything to do with his despising of his birthright (25:29–34). His rejection of his birthright reflects his character more than his personality, because he gives more importance to his physical needs rather than the spiritual blessings from God (Heb 12:16). Likewise, Jacob's preference to stay at home does not have anything to do with his being treacherous (Gen 27:36). His natural tendencies to cheat reflect his character, and not his personality.

Although some people prefer certain personality types over others, there is no such thing as a right or wrong personality. We are just different from one another, having different personality traits. Some types of personalities, it seems, are more prone to certain kinds of weakness. Among the sons of Jacob, for example, some are quick tempered like Simeon and Levi leading them to commit murder, while others are forbearing like Joseph which enables him to persevere in trials. Jesus's band of disciples also show varying types of personality, all of which have strengths and weaknesses.

As we discuss the various roles of a pastor for the remainder of this book, it is important to heed the reminder of Roy M. Oswald and Otto Kroeger:

> The pastoral ministry by its nature is a complex, demanding role, and our seminaries generally train people as though they must be competent in all its varied functions. Yet we believe there are few who can bring the excellence to *all* the functions of ministry demanded by the congregation.[8]

Aside from the varying gifts of those in ministry, one of the major factors is the pastor's personality. Understanding our nature is important, therefore. It helps us identify some of the potential weaknesses and strengths of having certain types of personality. Oswald and Kroeger further advise, "We have concluded that one person can never adequately fill the pastoral role—or at least the mythical role. What we can do is discover where our greatest strengths—and our greatest liabilities—lie and design the role accordingly."[9]

Peter Velander suggests that pastors with certain personalities thrive in ministries visible in the community while others do better as spiritual directors; there are those who are more inclined to be visionaries while others do better in managing building programs; some can excel as teachers while others can develop support groups; and some prefer that everything runs in an orderly fashion while others make decisions as they go along.[10] Seeing that different people have different personality traits should make the pastor appreciate the contribution of others in the building up of the body of Christ. Even though Paul was originally talking about various spiritual gifts when he uses the human body to illustrate the importance of every member of the church, this illustration is also appropriate in discussing the variety of personality types (1 Cor 12:15–26). If certain personality types do better in certain ministries, in the same way that the church needs people with different gifts, we can also say that the church needs people with various personality traits. This means that pastors must be willing to work with people of various personalities, because their strengths can complement ours.

Understanding our tendencies also allows us to make necessary adjustments when needed. Many pastors, for example, claim to be introverts. They naturally want to have less contact with people. However, pastoral ministry is about interacting with people, and not just with people, but with

---

8. Oswald and Kroeger, *Personality Type*, 27.
9. Oswald and Kroeger, *Personality Type*, 43.
10. Velander, "The Church Council," 4.

many people, usually more than any introverted person can handle. Some of them may even have overpowering personalities. Understanding our natural tendencies can help the pastors, not only to learn how to empathize with others, but also to identify the strengths and weaknesses of their personality so that they can trust God to use their strengths and overcome their weaknesses and be a better minister to others.

THE PASTOR AS A HUMAN

A common Chinese expression for pastor is 傳道人 (chuán daò rén), or "an evangelist." The three characters can be taken independently: 傳 means "to spread," 道 is "a teaching" or "moral principle," and 人 is "human." A pastor, therefore, is a person who spreads or propagates a moral principle or teaching. It is common to hear older Chinese pastors in the Philippines remind the younger ones that before they can propagate (傳) these moral teachings, they must first learn these moral principles (道); and learning these moral principles is, in essence, learning how to be human (人). A person who knows how to be human lives out these teachings.

Before thinking about being a pastor, one must learn what it means to be HUMAN:

- Humane: Be compassionate toward fellow humans.
- Upbringing: Understand our unique upbringing and how it affects us as a person.
- Manners: Learn proper manners, knowing that every culture has its own standards of propriety.
- Attitude: Humility is a universally accepted virtue, and pastors must all the more aim to have this quality.
- Nature: Know our personality traits, their potential weaknesses and strengths.

Questions for Personal Reflection

Humane: Are there certain types of people to whom you find it difficult to show compassion? If so, what types of people are they? What is the reason you find it difficult to show compassion to them (e.g., they belong to a different ethnic group or social class or religious affiliation)? What steps can you do to learn to be more compassionate toward them?

Upbringing: Reflect upon the way you were brought up. Do you notice any traits or habits or manners or outlooks in life that you think were influenced by the people that surround you as you grow up? Evaluate them according to the teachings of the Scripture. Are there things that need to change and what should you keep?

Manners: Consider the context in which you will serve or are serving. What actions or words are considered inappropriate, disrespectful, or lewd? Do you find yourself criticized for doing something people considered culturally inappropriate? Is there a tension between what is considered culturally appropriate and biblically sound? Or are they consistent?

Attitude: How can we distinguish between confidence and arrogance? How is arrogance displayed in the way we communicate with others, in our speech, in our actions? Think about instances when we are tempted to be arrogant. What are the reasons we may think we are better than others? Is it because of our affluence, achievements, affiliations, or appearance? How can we stay human and stay humble?

Nature: Have you identified your personality traits? What are the potential weaknesses and strengths of having these traits? How can you overcome or avoid these weaknesses? How can you enhance the strengths?

2

The Pastor as a Servant

Many who think of themselves as a servant-leader aren't—which amounts to self-deception. Many are tyrants, dictators, self-aggrandizers and benevolent oppressors. What sometimes passes for Christian leadership is rather shocking.[1]

—Duane Elmer

THE FUNDAMENTAL ROLE OF a pastor is to be a servant, first to God, and also to the people. The *essential function* of a pastor as servant is the foundation upon which all other roles are built. This means that the pastors assume their other roles because they are servants. They preach, teach, and make disciples as forms of service to edify the church; they counsel in order to serve those who need strength and encouragement; they evangelize in the service of those who need to hear the good news and do the work of an apologist to serve the flock by defending them from spiritual predators; they do theological reflections and interpret the Scripture to serve God's people by bringing the message God to them; they manage church affairs and their families to serve God's people by setting things in order; they lead the congregation in worship so that they can serve God

---

1. Elmer, *Cross-Cultural Servanthood*, 156.

as well; and they practice spiritual discipline not only to enhance their relationship with God but also to find strength as they continue serving the people. In other words, pastors can be counselors, disciple-makers, teachers/trainers, exegetes/prophets, evangelists/apologists, theologians/ethicists, managers, family persons, liturgists, and hermits only because they are servants.

In pastoral ministry, leadership is actually about servanthood. This begins with the pastor having the mindset of a servant and embodying this identity. Unless the pastor learns about servanthood, the most essential element of the pastoral ministry remains lacking. What do pastors as servants do? They SERVE! A pastor-servant is someone who is willing to Sacrifice, to Encourage their fellow ministers, to Respect everyone indiscriminately, to live out Christian Virtues to glorify God, and to Empower others so they can serve God as well.

SERVANTS SERVE

Sacrifice

The pastoral ministry is a sacred task, yet it is one of the vocations that can be appealing to people with narcissistic tendencies. R. Glenn Ball and Darrell Puls observe,

> Popular thinking has the pastor in church conflict as a target and victim of forces he or she cannot control. Over the course of time, we independently noted a large percentage of church conflicts where the pastor was the instigator and the issues centered on the pastor and his or her behaviors that included grandiosity, paranoia, rage, arrogance, lack of empathy, the inability to forgive, and his or her demands for appreciation, adulation, and compensation. The behaviors were self-destructive and nonsensical. In these cases, the pastor was indeed his own worst enemy.[2]

One who does sacred work is not necessarily serving God. Jesus prophesied about those who will claim to have healed the sick and exorcised, but he will reject (Matt 7:22–23). Simon the magician desired to do what the apostles did, but with ulterior motives (Acts 8:18–23). Likewise, not everyone who enters the pastorate should be in the ministry. Some enter the ministry even though they are not called to the ministry. Some enter it

2. Ball and Puls, "Narcissistic Personality Disorder in Pastors," 1.

because of the perquisites often attached to it, such as the respect and trust of the people, the impression of religiosity and spirituality, the visibility, the opportunity of speaking in front of a captured audience, and the spiritual authority one can exercise over another. Some think of the ministry as a means for personal advancement and a way of gaining or increasing their social capital. In this way, ministry becomes self-serving rather than a means to serve God by serving his people. Jesus, however, defines ministry differently. This is clear in his conversation with "the mother of the sons of Zebedee" (Matt 20:20).

Jesus was fully aware of his identity. In any red-lettered edition Bible, 74 of the 79 instances the expression "Son of Man" is used in the Gospels and Acts are in red (the exceptions: Mark 8:31; 9:9; John 12:34 [used twice]; Acts 7:56). This is how Jesus often referred to himself. Although it is a glorious title because it highlights his authority on earth (e.g., Luke 6:5), and future glory (e.g., John 5:27), associated with the title are his limitations as human (e.g., Matt 8:20), his earthly suffering (e.g., Mark 9:12). Jesus was fully aware of his task and the purpose for his coming (e.g., Luke 19:10). Although he knew the glory that awaits him and the authority that he would assume, he understood that sacrifice would precede them. In the Gospel of Matthew, for instance, Jesus predicted his sufferings and death several times (Matt 12:40; 17:12, 22; 20:18). He was willing to go through suffering because he knew the purpose of his coming, "even as the Son of Man came not to be served but to serve, and to give his life as a ransom for many" (20:28).

In a conversation with his disciples before his third prediction of his death, Jesus promised them that they would be rewarded with seats of authority in his kingdom (19:28). This, of course, raised the question as to which two disciples will be seated beside him. The mother of James and John must have learned about Jesus's promise, so she began to lobby for her two sons so they could receive the two highest honors among the Twelve (20:21). Jesus had to clarify to her that within God's kingdom, the most important question, especially for those who would be leading, is not who gets the highest position of authority.

The two brothers were with their mother when she made this request for them; and Jesus, turning to James and John, asked whether they would be able to go through the same sufferings he would go through (20:22). Although they answered affirmatively, Jesus did not give in to her request and pointed to God as the only one who can make decision about this matter (20:23). The other ten disciples were not happy with what happened, they might have been thinking of the same thing and were disappointed someone else asked for it first, and so Jesus had to remind them about the importance of servanthood (20:25–28).

To say that leadership is about servanthood sounds paradoxical, but this is the way taught by our Master whose purpose for coming was to serve (Mark 10:45). Leadership is not about who gets "promoted" to positions of authority. It is not about personal advancement, but about sacrifice. Jesus is the example of servanthood and sacrifice. Although he knew his authority and his true identity, but he also knew his purpose and the task given to him which is to be a servant. He was willing to serve by fulfilling the task given to him even if it means he had to offer himself as a sacrifice, his life as a ransom (Matt 20:28).

Encourage

No man is an island. Likewise, the pastoral ministry is a task for a team, not for an individual. Any local church needs more than one worker, whether all of them are full time or some of them are lay volunteers, one person cannot fulfill all the demands of the ministry. Pastors need coworkers, not only because the load of church ministry can be too heavy for one person to carry, but also because even pastors need encouragements. Even the first Christian church in Jerusalem initially have the apostles serving as its leaders, together with other unnamed elders (Acts 15:2, 4, 6, 22–23; 16:4). There may be times when, and for various reasons, there is only one pastor serving in a local congregation, but this is not ideal. A church minister needs other ministers, whether pastors/elders or deacons, to work alongside them. Jesus stresses that the pastoral ministry must be characterized by team spirit and encouragement.

The New Testament writers candidly recount the competition among the Twelve disciples. Luke, for example, talks about the dispute among the disciples as to who is the greatest among them (Luke 22:24). Jesus responded to this question by telling them that as followers of Christ, they ought to have a different standard of leadership (22:26). For Jesus, leadership is not about dominating others the way ancient benefactors exercise authority over their beneficiaries or the way rulers exercise lordship over his subjects. Jesus defined leadership and greatness in terms of service and servanthood, "The kings of the Gentiles exercise lordship over them, and those in authority over them are called benefactors. *But not so with you*. Rather, let the greatest among you become as the youngest, and *the leader as one who serves*. For who is the greater, one who reclines at table or one who serves? Is it not the one who reclines at table? But I am among you as the one who serves." (22:25–27, italics added).

The pastoral team must also be characterized by *mutual encouragement*. Luke shows that Peter has a more prominent role compared to the other disciples. After Jesus defined leadership as servanthood, he turned to Peter and informed him of the ongoing spiritual battle that could have caused his faith to fail, but assured him that through Jesus's prayer for him he would stand (22:31–32). After Jesus encouraged Peter, he instructed Peter, "strengthen your brothers" (22:32). As the leader of the group, Peter was given the responsibility to *encourage the others*. Interestingly, Peter had his weaknesses as well. Jesus revealed that he would later betray his teacher (22:33–34). As pastors, we may have our share of weaknesses, but these are not reasonable excuses for us to avoid being an encourager, especially to those who work with us.

Pastoral leadership is not a ministry for the perfect and "super-spiritual" people, but for those who understood and experienced the grace of God, and are willing to extend the same grace to encourage fellow workers. Jesus reminded his disciples that the real gauge of leadership is one's willingness to serve (22:26–27), and not the authority one has over others. Peter instructed the church leaders to set a good example by not "lording it over" the people under their care (1 Pet 5:1–3). His instruction to the believers shows that he remembered the example Jesus set to them and the instruction he gave him, "strengthen your brothers" (Luke 22:32).

How can we encourage our fellow workers? The stories of Barnabas illustrate the various ways we can strengthen others. Joseph of Cyprus, better known as Barnabas, often comes to mind whenever we talk about encouraging fellow workers. The few stories recorded in the Scripture about him shows that he deserved the nickname "Barnabas," which means "son of encouragement" (Acts 4:36–37). First, he encouraged others by sharing material possessions. Barnabas was first mentioned after he sold his land so that he can share material blessings with other believers, earning him the name "Barnabas" (4:36–37). As a result, "There was not a needy person among them" (4:34). Second, Barnabas stood by Paul, a former persecutor of Christians turned evangelist, and vouched for him before the other disciples in Jerusalem that he was truly a changed man. Paul wanted to join the Christians in Jerusalem but the disciples were afraid of him, but Barnabas defended him before the apostles and the believers in Jerusalem (9:27). Third, Barnabas took Mark with him when Paul refused to bring Mark with them on their mission trip. Mark withdrew the first time they went on a mission, so Paul thought it best not to bring Mark with them again (15:38). Paul and Barnabas had disagreements resulting in them going separate ways (15:39–41). Barnabas took Mark with him, and his efforts to encourage Mark clearly paid off. Paul later acknowledged Mark as a reliable coworker (2 Tim 4:11).

Respect

Respect is not only something we receive; it is also something we give. In his discussion about cross-cultural ministry, Elmer identifies several factors that limit a person's acceptance or respect of others: language (one's unwillingness to learn the language of others so as to communicate better), impatience (a desire to see things get done soon), ethnocentrism (the tendency to believe one's cultural values and traditions are better than others), category width (range of things we place in mental categories by which we make decisions), and dogmatism (the degree of rigidity with which we hold to our beliefs, cultural traditions, and personal preferences).[3] The same can be said even in the pastoral ministry. Our unwillingness to learn from others, sense of self-importance, and inflexibility often keep us from showing respect to others.

There are four important principles about respect that every minister must remember. First, *respect is something one earns*. This is an advice we often hear older ministers say to the younger pastors. There is no question that this is a sound and wise instruction. Remembering that respect is something earned keeps ministers from having that sense of entitlement. It also prevents us from being presumptuous and carefree with the way we live and behave. This is essentially what Paul was saying to Timothy when he said, "Don't let anyone look down on you because you are young, but set an example for the believers in speech, in conduct, in love, in faith and in purity" (1 Tim 4:12).

Paul's advice seems to suggest that there were people who considered Timothy's age as a point against him. In many cultures, youth is considered as a sign of inexperience and immaturity. Paul instructed his disciple not to allow other people's lack of respect deter him from doing what he ought to do as a minister. Instead, he must show that he is worthy of respect through his character. It is not for Timothy to demand respect from others, but he is to prove that he is worthy of respect through his words and actions, through his relationship with God and with others.

Second, *respect is something one must give willingly*. Paul's instruction to Timothy not only suggests that respect is something one earns, but it is something one gives willingly. Paul gave this advice to the young Timothy. However, Timothy would not be forever young. The command Paul gave

---

3. Elmer, *Cross-Cultural Servanthood*, 32.

the young Timothy should echo in the ears of the old Timothy, not to withhold respect from younger ministers until they "earned" it, but to willingly give it whenever he has the opportunity (3:2; see also 1 Pet 3:2). This is because respect is not only something we earn, but it is something we should generously give to others.

Moreover, it is not to be given only to fellow ministers, but also to everyone. Peter Short correctly observes,

> Learning to respect the people of the church is a good beginning place in ministry. It is remarkable how often we ministers view the people of our congregations as a problem to be dealt with... A pastor begins with respect for the people as the photographer begins with respect for the light. Just as an artist can "see" the work before it emerges from the materials, so the pastor learns to see what is within the people. This is heart work. The heart is what makes it possible for the eyes to see.[4]

It is natural for humans to find something that they have that others do not have (and vice versa) in making decisions who is worthy, less worthy, or unworthy of respect. For Paul, character is the determining factor to show that the person is worthy of respect. For many today, the person's talent and abilities, work experience, social status, educational attainment, eloquence and personality, language proficiency, race and ethnicity, denominational or theological affiliations, among others, are used as bases for making this decision. Oftentimes, even Christian ministers carry this attitude as we relate to other ministers and the people in our congregation. It is easy to find something about them that makes them less respectable, and this is used as an excuse to withhold respect.

The Scripture's instruction is clearly the opposite of our natural tendencies, "Honor one another above yourselves" (Rom 12:10). Oftentimes, we deprive others respect because we think we are better than them. No wonder Paul also said, "Do nothing from selfish ambition or conceit, but in humility count others more significant than yourselves" (Phil 2:3). Respect for others is, for Paul, like a tax obligation we owe others (Rom 13:7). Respect is not just something we earn; it is also something we give generously to others.

Third, *respect is something one may lose.* If it is something we can earn, it is something we can lose. It seems that our default is to *not show respect until the other person did something good enough to earn it*. What if we change our default to generously *show respect until the other person did something horrible enough to lose it*? This will definitely change the dynamics

---

4. Short, "Respect is the Beginning," 7–8.

of our ministry. There is a fourth principle that is in conjunction with the third, *respect lost is something one can regain*. If one can earn it, one can lose it; likewise, if one can lose it, one can regain it. The fact that Paul brought Mark the first time shows that he had respect for this young missionary (Acts 12:25). Paul clearly lost confidence in him after he abandoned the team (Acts 15:38); but Mark regained Paul's trust.

Virtues

Paul gave Timothy and Titus a list of qualities expected from a pastor/elder (1 Tim 3:1–7; Tit 1:1–9). Most of the qualities in his list were part of the moral expectations for every member of the ancient Greco-Roman society. One does not need to be a Christian pastor to value integrity, hospitality, goodness, sensibility, faithfulness, patience, and prudence. Even until now, most cultures have a set of moral expectations, and even though one culture may stress one quality more than the others, but these expectations from various societies are basically similar. This means that the virtues expected for simply being human are also expected from anyone who claims to be a follower of Jesus, and the same standards apply for those in the ministry.

One of the requirements for elders in Paul's list is that the elder must not be a recent convert "or he may become puffed up with conceit and fall into the condemnation of the devil" (1 Tim 3:6). Having too much too soon, for Paul, could result in arrogance; but this is not just the problem of newbies, it can be a perennial problem even for the older and more seasoned pastors. Elders who are arrogant are clearly not above reproach and respectable (3:2, 4); arrogance may also lead them to be violent, quarrelsome, and less dignified (3:3–4); such attitude can also affect the manner of teaching of the elders and their testimony before the "outsiders" (3:2, 7).

During the few years Jesus spent with his disciples, he taught them lessons about faith and piety, faithfulness and commitment, and love. There is one lesson that he repeatedly taught his disciples in connection with servanthood/leadership, and that is the lesson on humility. John made it clear that Jesus was fully aware of his mission and his identity, and that God had already given him divine authority. Aware of these, Jesus began to wash the feet of the disciples, "Jesus, knowing that the Father had given all things into his hands, and that he had come from God and was going back to God, rose from supper. He laid aside his outer garments, and taking a towel, tied it around his waist. Then he poured water into a basin and began to wash the disciples' feet and to wipe them with the towel that was wrapped around him" (John 13:3–5).

Jesus washed their feet for two reasons. First, it is symbolic of Judas's betrayal. In the same way that not every member of the body is clean, not every member of Jesus's group of disciples is "clean" (13:10–11). Jesus only washed the feet of those he considered to be a part with him (13:8), yet one of those who was part of him would betray him (13:18–19). Second, it exemplifies the virtue of humility which Jesus expected his disciples to imitate. Washing feet is not the responsibility of a teacher, it is the work of a slave. Jesus told Peter that the one who had bathed is already clean (13:6–10), but even after bathing, the feet easily get dirty especially when one travels by foot with open sandals, which was what Jesus and his disciples normally do. Yet instead of having a slave wash the feet of Jesus and his disciples, Jesus took the role of the slave to wash their feet for his disciples to imitate. He said to his disciples, "I have set you an example that you should do as I have done for you" (13:15). It is not the washing of feet per se that Jesus wants his disciples to imitate, but the virtue it expresses, namely, humility.

Humility, in this story, is the willingness to serve all kinds of people. Jesus also told his disciples, "Very truly I tell you, whoever accepts anyone I send accepts me; and whoever accepts me accepts the one who sent me" (13:20). These words were not addressed to the unbelieving world to remind them that they should receive the disciples he sent to them to preach the gospel. These words were addressed to the disciples who must welcome anyone Jesus sent to them. Just as Jesus accepted and washed the feet of everyone, even the one who would betray him, so also the disciples must receive and be willing to serve everyone. A humble leader does not choose the people he serves.

One final note about humility. Humility must be considered as an honorable virtue to acquire because it reflects the character of Christ, not as a temporary means to a greater end. Elmer puts it aptly:

> Some people tend to believe that humility is a means to an end—a stage we go through before deserving exaltation. We might be inclined to believe this from verses like "Whoever exalts himself will be humbled, and whoever humbles himself will be exalted" (Mt 23:12). Humility, however, isn't temporary; it isn't a training for the next level; it isn't a means to some higher end. Humility is a lifestyle, not isolated incidents. It is an attitude toward God, ourselves and others that permeates our thoughts and deeds. The Scripture says it this way: "Clothe yourself with humility" (1 Pet 5:5). When God sees a humble spirit, he may exalt that person. But God expects humility to continue to characterize that person's life. When it doesn't, God will humble him or her.[5]

---

5. Elmer, *Cross-Cultural Servanthood*, 32.

Empowerment

The use of the title "servant-leader" to refer to pastors may have been an attempt to correct abuses of some Christian leaders. A change of title or designation without a change of heart does not really do any good for the pastor.

Another version of the story Matthew recounts (20:20–28) is found in Mark. The two brothers clearly wanted to be the leaders of the group. A desire to lead, in itself, is not wrong. However, Jesus's response to James and John when the two asked Jesus to be next in the line to Jesus shows what was really at the heart of their desire to lead. Actually, the response of the ten other disciples also reveals what was in their hearts (Mark 10:41).

Jesus explained that the model of leadership common among the "rulers of the Gentiles" is not the one he wanted his disciples to follow. He explained that "the rulers of the Gentiles lord it over them, and their high officials exercise authority over them," but told his disciples, "Not so with you" (10:42–43). The command is clear—they should not lead by lording it over those under their authority, instead they are to lead by serving.

What does it mean to "lord it over" other people? The Greek word translated "lord it over" is *katakurieuō*. This word is seldom used in the New Testament; three of the four times are used in relation to leadership (Matt 20:25; Mark 10:42; 1 Pet 5:3), and the fourth one about a demon-possessed man physically *overpowering* many people (Acts 19:16). However, it is often used in the Greek Old Testament providing us a clearer idea about the meaning of the word. In some cases, it refers to one nation *conquering* another (Num 33:22, 29; Dan 11:39). In Psalm 110:2, it is used about the Messiah *subduing* his enemies, and in 10:9, about a lion *catching* its prey before eating them up. Sin is said to "lord it over" or to have *dominion* over humans (119:133), just like death has the ability to *overpower* humans leaving them no choice but to succumb (49:11). God may also *exercise authority* over a wayward son so he cannot continue in his wrong ways (Jer 3:14). In all these examples, even though the word *katakurieuō* may be translated differently, but they all have one thing in common. Those who "lord it over" others use their authority to *render others powerless*.

The pastoral relationship is sometimes seen today as a relationship between the dominant shepherd and the submissive sheep. As pastors, however, we need to remember that "*Shepherd* is much more an image of personal strength than one of dominance over lesser creatures."[6] When Jesus commanded his disciples not to "lord it over" others, it should be understood

---

6. Patton, *Pastor as Counselor*, 3.

as a prohibition to render others powerless. If we are to put this command positively, *the prohibition to "lord it over" others can also be considered a command to empower others.* "Lording it over" someone is not about being bossy or being a slave-driver; although these may be expressions of it, too. Pastors "lord it over" their coworkers and congregation if they do not equip them to serve, hence monopolizing the ministry and producing a personality-centered congregation. Senior pastors "lord it over" their associates if they do not allow them to thrive and excel by limiting their opportunities to serve. Church leaders "lord it over" their peers when their personal ambitions drive their activities to the point that they are ready to put others down in order to get ahead of the rest. Come to think of it, pride, insecurity, and selfishness are at the root of all these. This is the way the world works, but Jesus's warning is clear, "not so with you."

There will be instances when pastors should say *no* to ministry suggestions either because it is unnecessarily redundant or there are not enough resources for it to push through or it is simply inconsistent with the teachings of the Scripture. At times, pastors also need to say *no* to certain people being assigned to a particular work because of theological or character issues. However, pastors must also be constantly aware of their own struggles with insecurities, prejudice, selfishness, and pride. Pastors do not have to be an active barrier shrewdly fighting or violently opposing the work of their associates or members of their congregation to lord it over them. Most of the time, pastors just need to be a passive dead weight. Whenever we put unnecessary obstacles so that others are not empowered or deprived of the opportunity to serve, we may think that we are just being faithful to God, but according to Paul we are actually not serving God, "watch out for those who cause divisions and create obstacles . . . such persons do not serve our Lord Christ, but their own appetites" (Rom 16:17–18).

Donald A. Freeman identifies five characteristics of ministry; one of them is about empowering people.[7] He observes that we often overlook lay people who feel unempowered to minister in areas where they believe God wants them to serve. Empowering people means providing the necessary training and creating ministry opportunities for them. We will discuss more about this in the chapter on *The Pastor as Teacher/Trainer*.

THE PASTOR AS A SERVANT

Servanthood is at the core of the pastoral ministry. The English word "minister" is often used to translate both the Greek verb *diakoneō* ("to serve")

---

7. Freeman, "Five Important Characters of Ministry," 56.

and the noun *diakonos* ("servant"), and the word "ministry" is translated from *diakonia* ("service"). Ministry is service; to minister is to serve; and a minister is a servant. Jesus modeled servanthood as he led his disciples. His example is the one that every minister of the Gospel must imitate.

Pastors are ministers, and as servants, they do one thing—they SERVE! And there are various ways to do so:

- Sacrifice: Ministry is not always easy, and pastors must be willing to sacrifice for their sheep.
- Encourage: Ministry includes mutual encouragement from fellow ministers.
- Respect: Respect is not only something we earn; it is also something we give generously.
- Virtues: A servant must develop Christian virtues, and more importantly, the virtue of humility.
- Empower: Servanthood also requires the pastors to help others become servants of God.

Questions for Personal Reflection

Sacrifice: What was your reason for entering the pastorate? How did you confirm that God is calling you to the ministry? What sort of sacrifices do you have to make in order to enter the ministry? What sort of sacrifices do you have to make as you continue in the ministry? Do you think these sacrifices entitle you for something? Why or why not?

Encourage: What kind of struggles do you experience as one who wants to enter the ministry or as one who is already in the pastorate? To whom can you share these struggles so that they can pray for you? How can you strengthen your brothers/sisters as they go through difficulties while in the ministry?

Respect: What are some of the things that prevent you from showing respect to another person? Is it their age? Educational background? Social status? Lack of perceivable accomplishments? Ethnicity or race? Language? Physical appearance? Gender? If we perceive others as unworthy of respect because of any of these reasons, is the problem with their insufficiency or our attitude? If it is the latter, what can we do to correct our attitude?

Virtues: Do you agree that the lack of humility on our part is one of the major reasons we have difficulty showing respect to others? Recall instances when you are tempted to be proud or have shown pride, what motivates this kind of attitude? True humility starts from the heart and the way we view ourselves, but there are also many expressions of humility. In the context where you serve or will be serving as pastor, what are the expressions of humility?

Empower: Is there any reason that can keep you from empowering others in the ministry? Is it the fear that if we give others opportunity, they might do a better work than us? Is it our selfish ambition that we refuse to let others get involved because we wanted to get all the glory for doing the work? If we answer yes to any of the last two questions, what corrections do we need to make?

3

The Pastor as a Counselor

The shepherding metaphor reveals the care-giver in the role of a steady companion and patient guide of the soul, who constantly provides healthy nourishment for the soul. It is a consoling and refreshing image that combines and integrate diverse elements: nurture, wholesome feeding, leading, protecting and guarding the flock at rest.[1]

—Thomas C. Oden

One important role of the pastor is to be a counselor who takes care of the spiritual needs of the people. "Pastor" is another word for "shepherd," and the shepherd's task is not just to feed the sheep and protect them from danger, he must also help them find a place to rest, and care for them if they have special needs. Jesus often used the metaphor of sheep for his people. He commanded Peter to shepherd his flock (John 21:15–17), and Peter gave a similar instruction to the pastors of the churches (1 Pet 5:1–5). Consider the letters of Paul and the other New Testament writers, it is clear that even among believers, there are people who are hurting and need compassion, those who need rebuke (1 Cor 5:1–13), those who need encouragement (e.g., Heb 10:19–25), those who

1. Oden, *Classical Pastoral Care*, 1:41.

need affirmation (e.g., 1 Thess 1:2–3), and those who simply need to be reminded that someone cares for them (e.g., 1 Cor 16:24). While the New Testament writers cannot be with the believers personally, they used letters to pastor these churches.

As a counselor, the pastor's main responsibility is to care for the congregation, especially those with special needs. In the same way the shepherd cares for his sheep, the pastor CARES for the congregation. They do so by being Compassionate to those with needs, by being Authentic in the way they give care, by being Realistic so as not to give unnecessary promises and false hopes to the people, by being Empathetic, and by being Sensitive in administering care.

A COUNSELOR CARES

Compassionate

Compassion is one of the essential elements of the pastoral ministry. As David G. Benner explains, "Pastoral care is a ministry of compassion, its source and motivation being the love of God. It includes such things as visiting the sick, attending to the dying, comforting the bereaved, supporting those who are struggling or facing difficulties of any kind, preaching, and administering the sacraments."[2] Compassion can be expressed in various ways, but the bottom line is helping the people find comfort in times of pain. Phil C. Zylla defines compassion as "a desire to alleviate the sufferings of others."[3] Compassion is needed the most when a person goes through pain and suffering. We find Jesus's presence with suffering people as they go through crises. Bruce Petersen writes, "Nowhere was the extent of Jesus's compassion more evident than when he stood beside Mary and Martha, weeping as he stared at the tomb of his friend Lazarus."[4] Even in view of his impending death, Jesus tried to find ways to comfort his disciples by promising them the Holy Spirit (John 14:16–19).

The Gospels record several instances when Jesus had compassion on people. He had compassion on those who were sick (Matt 14:14), those who were hungry (Matt 15:32; Mark 8:32), the person oppressed by evil spirit (9:22), and the widow whose only son died (Luke 7:13). Interestingly, the verb rendered "show/have compassion" is *splanchnizomai* in Greek; this

---

2. Benner, *Care of Souls*, 189.
3. Zylla, "Inhabiting Compassion," 1.
4. Petersen, *Foundations of Pastoral Care*, 210.

word is related to *splanchnon* or "entrails,"⁵ which is used metaphorically by the ancient Greeks to refer to a person's innermost feelings. In short, compassion is something that comes from deep within a person as they are moved by the conditions of another.

In another story, Jesus went to several villages in Galilee teaching in the synagogues, preaching the kingdom of God, and healing the sick. Many people came to listen to his message and receive healing. Matthew continues, "When he saw the crowds, he had compassion for them, because they were harassed and helpless, like sheep without a shepherd" (9:36). Jesus's Jewish contemporaries believed that God would send his Messiah to rule his kingdom. Jesus and his disciples share the same belief, and so when the disciples preach Jesus as the Messiah, they were simply proclaiming Jesus to be the king who would rule as God's representative. Matthew tells a series of stories about the miracles performed by Jesus that shows that he was the Messiah (8:1–9:34). In the next chapters, Jesus instructed his disciples to preach (10:1–42); after which, he himself continued proclaiming the kingdom of God and performing the "deeds of the messiah" (11:1–2). In between these stories, Matthew recounts the incident when Jesus and his disciples were going through the cities and villages to preach in the synagogues of the Jews, and as he they did, Jesus felt *compassion* for the people because they were "like sheep without a shepherd" (9:36).

"Sheep without a shepherd" was how Moses described the Israelites if there is no one to lead them into the Promised Land (Num 27:17); and this was how the prophet Micaiah described the Israelite army when he foresaw the death of King Ahab in battle (1 Kgs 22:17; 2 Chr 18:16). This was also how Jesus described the Jews who needed the real king to reign over them. Shepherding is a form of leadership; and Jesus as the Chief Shepherd is to lead his people. There are people today who are still "like sheep without a shepherd," and that is because they have yet to acknowledge Jesus as king; and the pastor, as a counselor, can be instrumental in reminding the people that they have to live under God's rule. Human sufferings can be caused by a lot of things, but there are times when it results from our refusal to acknowledge Jesus as master. If this is the case, there is only one right thing to do, recognize Jesus as Lord.

Jesus is the king who invites us to be under his yoke, yet promises us that his yoke is easy and his burden is light (Matt 11:28–30). Keep in mind that the Jews were under the "yoke" of Romans, but unlike the Roman emperors who ruled with tyranny, Jesus the Messiah felt *compassion* toward the people. It is compassion that led Jesus to tell his disciples, "The

5. BDAG, s.vv. "*splanchnizomai*," "*splanchnon*."

harvest is plentiful but the workers are few. Ask the Lord of the harvest, therefore, to send out workers into his harvest field" (9:37–38). As Jesus sent out his disciples after this conversation, he basically instructed them to do the works he was doing—proclaim that God is king and do acts of mercy (10:5–8). His workers are expected to have the same compassion that Jesus showed the people.

The pastors as counselor should not only proclaim the same message that Jesus instructed his disciples to proclaim, but they should also show the same kind of compassion Jesus showed the people who needed to acknowledge him as king.

Authentic

It is natural for church members to expect their pastors to be spiritually strong leaders. Actually, it is right for them to have such expectations because pastors are their spiritual leaders; but pastors, just like any follower of Jesus, have their share of weaknesses. The expectation to be perfect makes it more difficult for the pastor to be authentic. Barbara J. Blodgett has high hopes for ministers despite such pressure as she writes:

> Ministers have for so long been expected to be faultless—even in realms lying outside their ministerial work—and this sometimes leads them to try to be people they are not. Many especially feel as though they should be the superheroes of the faith. Someone once coined the phrase "super Christian" to denote a religious leader's responsibility to be perfect human being. (After all, it is not only children who sometimes mistakes clergy for God.) In the face of such an unrealistic expectation, ministers have often cowered. And yet I believe clergy dearly desire to be more themselves, less what others might want them to be.[6]

Church members do not only need someone who can lead them spiritually, they also need someone with whom they can identify and whose life can encourage them to say, "If God can work in the life of my pastors, weak as they are, he can work in my life as well." The author of Hebrews understood this principle very well. No wonder he assures the believers that we do not have a high priest, Jesus, who is aware of the difficulties we are facing, because just like us, he was tempted and went through much pain in life. Although he was without sin, he is one who can sympathize with our weaknesses and he can help us through our difficulties (Heb 4:14–16).

---

6. Blodgett, *Becoming the Pastor You Hope to Be*, 82.

The New Testament writers have no qualms showing Jesus as one who struggled with temptation (Matt 4:1–11; Luke 4:1–13), who shared both the joys (10:21) and pains (John 11:35) of humans, whose devotion to God caused deep indignation (Matt 21:12–13; Mark 11:15–18; Luke 19:45–48), who agonized in the face of death (Matt 26:39, 42; Mark 14:34–36; Luke 22:42; Heb 5:7), and who genuinely loved people (Mark 10:21). All these clearly show that Jesus was one who understood the experiences of humans. Knowing this should assure us that he is able to help us navigate through life.

Believers also need to know that their pastors share the same struggles they have as a testimony of God's grace. It shows that the pastor, like every disciple of Christ, having experienced God's guidance learned to help the believers through their difficult experiences. On the one hand, it is unwise for pastors to *constantly* discuss their weaknesses before the congregation. Doing so will not really help build up the church, but may discourage the believers and create doubts in their minds about the goodness and power of God. Oden warns the pastors/counselors against compulsive self-disclosure and advises, "Simple honesty was highly valued. One need not say everything in order to say what is pertinent. There was no absolute requirement that one ought to tell everything one knows about oneself."[7] On the other hand, giving the congregation the impression that in life, we can be free from struggles may result in more damage. Pastors who only talk about their experiences of victories can give the congregation a false sense of hope, discourage the believers whose life is not as "smooth" as that of their pastors, and make them blame themselves unnecessarily for having an imperfect life. There is really no reason for pastors to deny that they share the weaknesses of the rest of humanity. Authenticity tempered by wisdom is a key to a healthy ministry.

Just like Paul, pastors must be able to honestly say to their congregation, "Who is weak, and I do not feel weak? Who is led into sin, and I do not inwardly burn? If I must boast, I will boast of the things that show my weakness. The God and Father of the Lord Jesus, who is to be praised forever, knows that I am not lying" (2 Cor 11:29–31). This is another way of saying, "Yes, I do struggle just like you, but in my weakness, God is my strength, and as he helped me during my times of struggle, he can help you, too."

Realistic

There will be instances when members of our congregation come to us because they are going through crisis in life. Thus, the pastor must be ready

---

7. Oden, *Classical Pastoral Care*, 3:24.

to take the role of a counselor. Gary R. Collins proposes four things every counselor must consider when counseling: (1) the real problem of the counselee because what is presented may not be the real issue; (2) whether the counselor should try to help; (3) what can be done to help; and (4) is there another person more qualified to help.[8] Pastors doing counseling work must also ask the same questions. The second and fourth questions are good reminders for pastors that there are cases when the best help they can give is by not being directly involved. There is no question that God is ultimately the healer and helper of people who need care, but God can also use professionals to help restore a person's mental, psychological, and emotional health. This is something that not all pastors are trained to do.

The needs of the members of the congregation vary. Two sick members may ask the pastor to pray for them, one has a headache for lack of sleep, while the other is diagnosed with cancer. Two teenagers may seek the pastor's advice, one wanted to make sure he picked the right degree and school for college, while the other one is contemplating suicide. Two pairs of couples may approach the pastor for counsel, the first pair wanted the pastor's suggestion what to name their first child, while the second is at brink of separation. Two fathers may need help because of their sons, one has a son who spends too much time playing computer games, while the other one has a son addicted to drugs. Two mothers may be worrying about their daughters, one has a daughter who has a crush on her Math teacher and cannot concentrate on her studies, while the other suspects that her husband is molesting their daughter. Some problems are more complex than others and we do not have to be in the ministry for a long time to realize that there are some situations that are beyond the pastor's ability to help, and they should encourage their members to seek professional help.

There are limitations to what a pastor can do to help their church members. The encounter between the beggar who was born lame and the two apostles, Peter and John, can illustrate this (Acts 3:1–10). While they were on their way to the temple, they met this lame beggar who asked for alms. The ancient Jews considered the almsgiving as a religious duty, yet instead of giving him what he asked for, Peter said to him, "Silver or gold I do not have, but what I do have I give you. In the name of Jesus Christ of Nazareth, walk" (3:6). Like Peter, we can only give what we have, and pastors need to be realistic with regard to the extent of help we can offer the people. This may sound discouraging, but this is only half of the story. Peter admitted that he could not give what he did not have, but he also said that there is something else that he could offer, and he gave it freely. Although the story

---

8. Collins, *Christian Counseling*, 17.

is about the risen Lord working through the apostles and about God being the only source of healing, one should not miss an important point in the story—*we cannot give what we do not have*. Peter was unable to give what he did not have at that moment. Likewise, pastors cannot give what they do not have. Pastors who are not trained to provide professional help cannot (and should not!) give professional help.

Being realistic is also related to the pastor's integrity. Many members of the congregation do not really understand what the pastors are trained to do and what they are not trained to do. The assumption is that pastors, being the spiritual leader of the church and someone who is "closer" to God than anyone in the congregation, must be able to find ways to help any member with a special need. This assumption is clearly incorrect. Bill Blackburn observes that most people "appreciate the pastor's being honest in confessing a lack of training, background or time to deal with the particular issue being faced."[9] There will be occasions when the best help that the pastors can give is to refer the people seeking counseling to trained counselors. Referring members to professionals is a form of good pastoral care. This means that the pastors must also (1) know the variety of professionals to whom they would refer the counselees, (2) explain clearly to the counselees that the reason for the referral is the pastor's own limitations, (3) help the counselee to get in touch with the counselor, (4) reassure the counselees that they are not being rejected, (5) encourage the counselees by praying for them, and (6) continue to have contact with the professional to update the counselee's situation.[10]

Pastors need to be realistic and be aware of their own limitations. There are times when we may need to refer our members to someone who can better help them with their needs, but let us not forget the real Comforter who can truly bring peace to our lives, the one in whose name we minister to the congregation.

Empathetic

Pastors are not superhumans without frailties. As discussed above, because we share many of the struggles and weaknesses with the members of the congregation, there is really no reason for pastors to give the people an impression that they are above the people in this regard. Looking at this from a more positive viewpoint, our shared weaknesses and struggles make us

---

9. Blackburn, "Pastors Who Counsel," 80.
10. Blackburn, "Pastors Who Counsel," 80–81.

better equipped to empathize and understand the difficulties that the members experience.

The English word "empathy" comes from two Greek words: *en* (or "in") and *pathos* (or "suffering"). This suggests that to empathize is to identify with others in their suffering or to suffer together with them (or "sympathy"). Paul looked at his sufferings this way. Paul candidly talked about his sufferings with the Corinthian believers. Despite his sufferings, he was thankful to God because he was confident that God can comfort him and with the comfort he received from God, he would be able to comfort those who were going through sufferings. Thus, he told the Corinthians, "Praise be to the God and Father of our Lord Jesus Christ, the Father of compassion and the God of all comfort, who comforts us in all our troubles, so that we can comfort those in any trouble with the comfort we ourselves receive from God. For just as we share abundantly in the sufferings of Christ, so also our comfort abounds through Christ." (2 Cor 1:3–5).

Empathy requires understanding, understanding requires listening, and listening requires genuine care. The pastor who genuinely cares for his flock will take the necessary steps to listen and understand, not just the feelings and thoughts of the member, but also their situation and condition. No wonder Paul would send messengers to visit the believers whenever he was unable to visit them. For example, he sent Epaphras to Colossae, not only to inform the church how he was doing (Col 1:7–8; 4:7–9), but also to receive news about the Colossian believers (1:4). He did the same for the Corinthian, Thessalonian, and Philippian churches by sending Timothy (1 Cor 4:17; Phil 2:19; 1 Thess 3:2). Paul would also take time to listen to church members who would update him about the condition of the church. For example, members of Chloe's household informed Paul about the quarrels happening in the Corinthian church (1 Cor 1:11). He considered their report as valid and their action as evidence of their concern for the members of the church. With his authority, he took the necessary actions to help the believers settle their quarrels.

Reading the psalms is a good starting point in learning how to be empathetic. The psalms provide a wide range of expressions of pain brought by the various experiences of hardships. There are instances when the psalmist was being led to do what is wrong (Ps 5:8–10), grieved because of the hardships caused by his enemies (6:6–7), suffered because some people intentionally plotted to harm him (7:13–15), shamed by his enemies who gloated at his misery (13:1–2; 137:1–4), slandered (17:1–5; 64:1–5; 140:1–5), mocked (22:5–7), weighed down by guilt (25:18; 32:3–4; 38:1–22), accused falsely (27:12; 35:20), betrayed by close friends (41:5–9), struggled with doubt (44:8–14), overwhelmed by his enemies (55:2–7), weakened by his difficult circumstances (61:1–3; 69:1–5; 142:3; 143:4), tortured by the thought of injustice (73:1–28; 94:4–6), and felt abandoned by God (74:1–3; 79:8–11). Although people who go through sufferings respond to difficulties in various ways, reading through these psalms allows the pastors to get a glimpse of what could be going through the mind of people experiencing certain types of sufferings and the kinds of questions they may be asking. Empathy begins with understanding humans, and being humans ourselves, we should already have something in us with which we can identify with the pains of the members of the congregation.

Seward Hiltner stresses the importance of genuine engagement between the pastors as counselor and the members being counseled.

> [The] counselor needs some genuine warmth of personality, the ability to convince his parishioner that he is genuinely interested in him and to have this true in fact, the capacity to lay aside temporarily his own problems and concentrate understandingly on the person and problems of the parishioner, and the ability to retain his sensitivity to the nuances of communication.[11]

The leads us to the fifth characteristic that pastors as counselors must have—sensitivity.

Sensitive

Job's complaint against his friends expresses clearly what anyone going through crisis wanted to say, "Worthless physicians are you all. Oh that you would keep silent, and it would be your wisdom!" (Job 13:4b–5). An important reminder to every pastor/counselor: not all sufferings are direct consequences of the sins of the one who suffers. Jesus made this clear to his disciples when they asked him about the blind man who was born blind (John 9:2–3). In the case of the blind man, he was blind neither because of his own sin nor because of the sins of his parents, but because it would be an occasion for God's work to be seen. There may be cases when the pastor must be ready to gently confront sin when it is clearly the reason for a person's sufferings. However, in many cases, people suffer because of the sins of others or because of some unidentifiable reason. What the pastor/counselor can offer in situations like this are listening ears.

Every member of the congregation is unique. Having come from different backgrounds, having different gifts and abilities, having different set of experiences, having different conditions at present, each of them does not

11. Hiltner, *The Counselor in Counseling*, 163.

only have something unique to contribute in building up the church, each has a unique set of needs as well. Knowing the sheep is what Jesus does as the good shepherd (10:14); and it should be the aim of the pastor to be like our Great Shepherd who understands the needs of his sheep. It is practically impossible for one pastor to know every member's needs, especially in medium or large congregations; and therefore, help is needed in situations like this. Yet the fact remains, the shepherd must be sensitive to the needs of his flock.

Some of these needs can be addressed in the pulpit, while others require a more personal interaction. Yet in both cases, the Scripture should be the guide for those who face various challenges in life. Jesus used preaching to address some of these human needs, and in other cases, he had personal interactions with them.

Earlier, I briefly discussed the four questions proposed by Collins that every counselor must ask. The first question concerns the *real problem* of the counselee.[12] There will be instances when the person does not verbally communicate the real issue. This requires sensitivity on the part of the pastor. Although Richard Dayringer admits that "reading" a person is not an easy task, nonetheless, he stresses the importance of understanding the person being counseled, "One of the pastoral counselor's characteristic mark is sensitivity to people's hopes, fears, and tensions. Pastoral counselors must be particularly sensitive to all the little expressions of character such as posture, facial expression, dress, and apparently accidental movements of the body. Learn to read character."[13] There is, of course, danger in this kind of "reading," and the pastor as counselor must be aware of its limitations. However, there remains a need for pastors to be sensitive to those things that are not verbally communicated. This is what Jesus did when he communicated with the Samaritan woman. He went beyond what was verbally communicated to identify the real problem the woman was facing.

John shares about the time when Jesus went from the region of Judea to Galilee, and we are told that Jesus thought it was necessary to go through Samaria. The region of Samaria is in between the regions of Judea and Galilee. The shortest route between them is via Samaria; but for social and religious reasons, ancient Jews refused to pass through Samaria and would rather travel longer to avoid having contact with Samaritans (4:9). Jesus went through Samaria, not because he wanted to take a short cut, but because there was someone to whom he wanted to minister. By taking a shorter route, he was actually walking an extra mile. He did what a typical

---

12. Collins, *Christian Counseling*, 17.
13. Dayringer, *The Heart of Pastoral Counseling*, 77.

Jew of his time would not normally do, to minister to a Samaritan woman. As he ministered to her, he was able to direct their conversation so that he could address the special need of the woman. John did not give much details about the Samaritan woman's past marriages except that by the time Jesus was talking with her, she already had five failed relationships and she was living with a man who was not her husband. Jesus offered to quench her thirst, not her physical thirst, but her spiritual thirst (4:13–14). Apparently, the symptom of the woman's spiritual thirst was her moving from one relationship to another. Jesus did not just address the symptom, but he offered a longer lasting solution for her problem, which only he can give. This brings us back to one important truth that pastors need to remember as they minister to people with special needs, that the real source of satisfaction comes with having a relationship with God.

THE PASTOR AS A COUNSELOR

Crises and tragedies are common part of life; pain and grief are common experiences of humans, and Christians are not exempted from these. The members of the congregation also go through difficulties in life. It is not the responsibility of the pastors to solve the problems of the members of their congregation, but the pastor as a counselor can walk alongside those in pain, hoping that their presence can bring some comfort to the grieving.

The pastor as a counselor CARES for his flock. As they do, they must remember a few important things about giving care.

- Compassionate: Show compassion to those with special needs.
- Authentic: The pastor as counselor is not exempt from pain, and it brings comfort to the people to know that their shepherds also experience the challenges they experience.
- Realistic: Part of being realistic is the pastor's willingness to admit their limitations so as not to give false hopes to their congregation.
- Empathetic: The sheep naturally listen to the voice of their pastors, but the pastors must also be willing to listen to the cries of their sheep.
- Sensitive: Pain is often hard to communicate verbally. Thus, the pastor as a counselor must learn to listen carefully by being sensitive to what their sheep is communicating.

Questions for Personal Reflection

Compassionate: Do you find it difficult to show compassion to certain types of people? If so, in your observation, what type of people are they? Why do you think it is difficult for you to show compassion toward them?

Authentic: On a scale of 1–10 (1 being extremely uncomfortable and 10 being extremely comfortable), how comfortable are you sharing your weaknesses with your congregation? Do you see any repercussions for being open or being tight? How do you balance authenticity with wisdom?

Realistic: Consider the kind of trainings (both formal and informal) that you have received so far, how prepared are you to help the members of your congregation going through crisis in life? If you encounter difficult cases that you are unable to deal with, do know of anyone who can help them?

Empathetic: Paul says that the comfort he found after his own experiences of sufferings equipped him so he can comfort others who needed comfort (2 Cor 1:3–6). Do you see your own experiences of suffering as part of your training so you can be better equipped to comfort others? If so, in what ways?

Sensitive: The ability to listen to what is communicated verbally and non-verbally is essential in the ministry. What specific steps can you do to improve your listening skill? Is there anything in your life that could potentially hinder you from listening carefully?

4

The Pastor as a Disciple-Maker

I have proposed that there is a crisis at the heart of the local church. The integrity of the church's product is in jeopardy, therefore, threatening the mission and turning the present church environment into a hotbed of weakness. I have also proposed that the top priority for corrective is to rediscover and deploy the disciple-making pastor.[1]

—Bill Hull

THE ESSENTIAL PRINCIPLE FOR discipleship was explained by Paul to Timothy: Timothy should teach whatever he learned from Paul to faithful people who were expected to teach others as well (2 Tim 2:2). This task is for every believer; the expression "faithful men" (Greek, *pistois anthropois*) may refer to the faithful (that is, reliable/devoted) people, but it may also be translated as "people who belong to the faith." The goal of which is to see them teach others as well.

Let us not forget, however, that the task of initiating this work was given to Timothy, the pastor of the church in Ephesus. There are many ways to disciple others; some do it one-on-one, others do it in small groups; some informally, others more systematic; some short-term, other for a longer

---

1. Hull, *The Disciple-Making Pastor*, 97.

period. The goal of discipleship, however, is not going through a set of materials or finishing a certain course of study (although these are helpful), but to see every believer instructed in the ways of God and helping them to live their lives accordingly (Col 1:28), with that hope that they may be able to impart the life of Christ to others. As the pastors take on the role of a disciple-maker, they must LEARN: Listen to God and practice obedience, Explain the Scripture to their disciples and "teach them to obey," Admonish the believers to do what is right, Reproduce their lives in others so they can make disciples as well, and Nurture their disciples and help them experience life transformation.

DISCIPLE-MAKERS LEARN

Listen

How can we start going about this? It begins with listening. We can give instructions to others only if we receive God's instructions first. The prophet Isaiah shows us how this process begins:

> The Lord GOD has given Me the tongue of disciples,
> That I may know how to sustain the weary one with a word.
> He awakens *Me* morning by morning,
> He awakens My ear to listen as a disciple.
> The Lord GOD has opened my ear;
> And I was not disobedient
> Nor did I turn back. (Isa 50:4–5, NASB)

In Isaiah 50, the prophet was talking about God's Servant through whom he would redeem his people. The New Testament points to Jesus as the Servant in Isaiah. Isaiah describes the Servant's suffering this way, "He was oppressed, and he was afflicted, yet he opened not his mouth; like a lamb that is led to the slaughter, and like a sheep that before its shearers is silent, so he opened not his mouth" (Isa 53:7). When the Ethiopian eunuch asked Philip who this was, "Philip opened his mouth, and beginning with this Scripture he told him the good news about Jesus" (Acts 8:35). In short, the Suffering Servant is the same one who was sacrificed for human sins. Moreover, Jesus took upon himself Israel's role as "light to the nations" (Isa 49:6). The prophet Isaiah refers to Israel as the Servant who is also the "light to the nations" (49:6). In Simeon's prayer, he acknowledged Jesus as this "light," "Lord, now you are letting your servant depart in peace, according to your word; for my eyes have seen your salvation that you have prepared in the presence of all peoples, a light for revelation to the Gentiles, and for glory to your people Israel" (Luke 2:29–32). The light to the Gentiles (Greek, *ethnos*; can also be translated "nations") is the same one who commanded his disciples to make disciples of all nations (Matt 28:18–20).

The Gospel writers tell us that it was Jesus's custom to regularly commune with God (Mark 1:39; Luke 22:39). Isaiah said the same thing about the Servant, who listens to God "morning by morning," and the message he received from God is the same message he shared to "sustain the weary." Whatever the Servant learned from the Lord, he taught the weary; and he taught only what he learned from the Lord.

The process of discipleship involves imitation. This is essentially how Jesus described his relationship with the Father (John 5:19). Rowan Williams describes Jesus's relation to the Father:

> There is a connection in John's Gospel between the way in which disciples are to see and do what their Master is doing, and what Jesus himself says about his relation to the Father. If you look at John 5:19–20, you find one of the Gospel's great affirmations of how the Son does what the Father is doing because the Son sees what the Father is doing. The Son gazes on and absorbs the eternal action of the Father, and acts it out in his own life, in eternity and in history. The Son, the Word of God, drinks in the everlasting act of the Father and then makes it real in another context.[2]

Jesus the Servant was able to make others disciples of the Lord because he himself was a disciple of the Lord. This is the same principle applied by Paul to Timothy—he first taught Timothy, then expects Timothy to teach others, and then expects Timothy's students to teach others. Conversely, Timothy was able to teach others because he was, first of all, a disciple himself. Paul also instructed the Corinthians to imitate him as he imitates Christ (1 Cor 11:1).

God can teach his disciples through a number of means. He communicates through his word and through our prayers. The fact that the Servant communicated with God "morning by morning" (Isa 50:4) and Jesus consistently prayed "while it was still dark" (Mark 1:35) does not mean that early morning is the only time we should be communicating with God. Evening prayers (Ps 4) is just as good as morning prayers (Ps 5), and meditation of God's word is something we do "day and night" (Josh 1:8; Ps 1:2), not just on certain times of the day.

---

2. Williams, *Being Disciples*, 13.

Listening to God is required of someone who wanted to be a disciple-maker. The Servant listened, not only to have a message for those who are weary (Isa 50:4), but also to receive instructions from the Lord and do what he was instructed to do. Thus, he says, "I was not disobedient" (50:5). Making disciples includes "teaching them to obey" (Matt 28:20), and obedience should begin with the one who is making disciples.

Explain

Listening to God should result in obedience, and obedience to God is an important requirement for the disciple-maker who wants to "teach others to obey" (Matt 28:20). Teaching others to obey includes explaining to them *how* to obey. The analogy between a pastor and a coach has become popular in the recent years. Hull explains their similarities this way: "The pastor tells people what and why, then must assist people to put the teaching into practice . . . Jesus taught the disciples many things. What He taught them is vital; how He taught them is crucial as well."[3] He proceeds to explain the six steps Jesus used in teaching his disciples: (1) tell them what; (2) tell them how; (3) show them how; (4) do it with them; (5) let them do it; and (6) deploy them.[4] Our discussion in this section will focus on the second of these six steps. Jesus taught his disciples how to obey by explaining the Scripture to them.

The disciples of Jesus had a special privilege, not only of hearing Jesus taught firsthand, but also of receiving explanation to many of Jesus's teachings that are not easy to understand. The "crowd" in the Gospels may have had the opportunity to listen to the teachings of Jesus, but the disciples were privileged to hear more from him. There are things Jesus explained to his disciples that he did not tell to the crowd. The Sermon on the Mount is one example. After teaching in Galilee, Decapolis, and Judea (4:25), Jesus left the crowd together with his disciples to whom he explained the Scripture.

Explaining the Scripture is an essential element in disciple-making. Jesus took time explaining God's word to his disciples, not only by telling them what God expected from them as he did in the Beatitudes, but also by correcting traditional or popular understanding of the Scripture that is not consistent with its teaching. Hence, Jesus claimed to fulfill the Law, instead of rendering it useless (5:17). Jesus was not against the teachings of Moses; he was against the teachings of some Jews who gave more importance to their tradition than the teaching of the Scripture. Jesus went on to issue a

---

3. Hull, *Disciple-Making Pastor*, 243.
4. Hull, *Disciple-Making Pastor*, 243–44.

series of challenges against traditional understanding of the Law introduced by the statement, "You have heard that it was said to those of old . . . But I say to you" (5:21–22, 27–28, 31–32, 33–34, 38–39, 43–44).

Jesus was not against upholding traditions. In the first place, truth is preserved through tradition. If a tradition preserves the teachings of the Scripture, the only right thing to do is to continue handing it down. On many occasions, Jesus gave importance to tradition. For instance, after healing a leper, Jesus instructed him to offer the sacrifices prescribed in the Law (8:4). His practice of visiting the synagogue on Sabbaths also shows that Jesus honors good traditions. However, Jesus was against traditions that are inconsistent with the teachings of the Scripture; and this is one of the things he explained to his disciples.

Jesus explained to his disciples that God's commandments are more than just specific instructions and prohibitions. Instead, they are principles that are applicable to various situations and following these principles requires a person to start with the heart. No wonder Jesus taught against hypocrisy to show that evil actions are not the only ones springing out from an evil heart, but even good actions such as almsgiving, prayer, and fasting can be done with wrong motives (6:1–8, 16–18). As the disciple-maker, Jesus explained the importance of the state of one's heart. He showed that there is more to murder than just taking another person's life; the anger in one's heart has a lot to do with it. He showed that there is more to adultery than having extramarital affairs; the lust in one's heart has a lot to do with it. He showed that there is more to marriage and divorce than just a certificate to prove one's marital status; faithfulness has a lot to do with it. He showed that there is more to oaths than pronouncing them before others; the intention of one's heart is what really counts. He showed that retaliation and hatred are not solutions to quarrels; loving one's enemies is the better option. Jesus the disciple-maker taught his disciples the importance of one's heart. When what we say does not match what we do, it is considered hypocrisy; and when our main concern in doing the right thing is to appear right, that is also hypocrisy. Real obedience to God comes from within. Hence, Jesus challenged the tradition about obedience that focuses only on the appearance rather than transformation.

Admonish

Jesus commanded his disciples to "be perfect" (Matt 5:48). The English word "perfect" (Greek, *teleios*) can cause some confusion because the expression can mean flawless in appearance or sinless in character. In this life, there is no way one can ever attain the state of sinlessness, but it is possible to continuously grow to maturity. Maturity should be every believer's goal. The Greek word *teleios* can mean "perfect" in the sense of being "mature" or "complete." The instruction of James to endure hardship can shed some light to Jesus's command to be perfect. Enduring hardships, according to James, as a way for the believers to "be perfect and complete, lacking in nothing" (Jas 1:4b). Perfection means to lack nothing; conversely, imperfection means to lack something. No wonder in the verse that follows, James advises, "If any of you lacks wisdom, let him ask God, who gives generously without reproach" (1:5a). Being wise is being mature; lack of wisdom is lack of maturity or being imperfect. Wisdom, in this case, is not just knowing the right thing, but it is knowing and doing the right thing. As the believers grow in wisdom, they increasingly reflect God's character in their life. Paul also talks about the hardships we face in life as a means to "be conformed to the image of his Son" (Rom 8:29). Hardships teach us humility, dependence upon God, and perseverance; and learning these characters allows us to take one step closer to becoming like Jesus. Maturity or perfection, then, refers to becoming like Christ in character. This is what Paul desired every believer to attain.

The pastor has an important role in the believer's quest to maturity. Knowing that every believer must aim to become more like Christ, Paul saw his role of proclaiming Christ (which includes both admonishing and teaching) as an essential necessity. Admonition can be done to a group of believers, like what Paul did when he wrote his earlier letter to the Corinthians with the purpose of correcting wrong behaviors. He writes, "I do not write these things to make you ashamed, but to admonish you as my beloved children" (1 Cor 4:14). Admonition can also be done with a smaller group or with individuals. The goal is to encourage good conduct by correcting or discouraging wrong behaviors.

Pastors are not the only ones who have the responsibility to admonish others. Every believer is called to admonish one another (Rom 15:14; Col 3:16), but the pastor has a responsibility to take the lead. Greg Ogden identifies three essential elements necessary in helping others grow to maturity:

> *Relational vulnerability* means honest, self-disclosing and confessional relationships that give the Holy Spirit permission to remake us. Second, the *centrality of truth* is emphasized when people open their lives to one another around the truth of God's Word and the Lord begins to rebuild their lives from the inside out. And third, *mutual accountability* is authority given to others

to hold us accountable to mutually agreeable standards—"iron sharpening iron."[5]

Admonishing and teaching are important responsibilities of the pastors in order that the believers under their care may grow in maturity (Col 1:28). There are several areas in which believers needed admonition. Paul admonished the Ephesian elders to guard against false teachers. Before leaving Ephesus, Paul warned the elders of the church against the "savage wolves" who had been teaching perverse things (Acts 20:29–31). Likewise, with the hope of correcting wrong behaviors, Paul instructed the Thessalonians to admonish the unruly (1 Thess 5:14). He did the same concerning the lazy ones. After instructing the Thessalonians not to be idle but to earn their own living, he advised the believers (2 Thess 3:14–15).

Paul did not only teach and admonish the congregation; but as the more seasoned worker, he also took the responsibility to warn younger pastors like Timothy and Titus against false teachers (1 Tim 4:1; Tit 1:10), to make sure that they watch their life and teachings (1 Tim 1:3–4; 4:16). Proclaiming Christ requires admonition and teaching (Col 1:28). The pastor must do both, not only with his congregation, but also with his coworkers with the goal of seeing every believer mature in their faith. This requires the pastor to continuously grow toward maturity as well.

Reproduce

The idea of reproducing one's life in others is clear in Paul's command to Timothy, "and what you have heard from me in the presence of many witnesses entrust to faithful men, who will be able to teach others also" (2 Tim 2:2). This idea, however, was not a product of Paul's innovative genius. Jesus had already done it and instructed his disciples to do the same. Jesus spent only a little over three years doing public ministry on earth, and within that short period of time, he reproduced himself so that there would be more people like him ministering to others. This process of "reproduction" is what some would refer to as "disciple-making." He made disciples and commanded them to make disciples. Jesus expected his disciples to not only do the works that he did, but to do even more (John 14:12). He did so by instructing them to do four things: *learn his character, observe his deeds, understand his vision, and do the same thing.*

First, Jesus instructed his disciples to learn his character, "Take my yoke upon you, and learn from me, for I am gentle and lowly in heart, and

---

5. Ogden, *Discipleship Essentials*, 21.

you will find rest for your souls" (Matt 11:29). Even in the story of the washing of the feet of the disciples, Jesus instructed them to follow his example (John 13:13–15). Likewise, in writing to the Corinthians and Thessalonians, Paul boldly called them to imitate him as he imitates Christ (1 Cor 4:16; 11:1; 1 Thess 1:6). Pastors today must aim to do the same. By setting a good example before their flock despite imperfections, and by trusting the grace of God through their limitations, the pastor as a disciple-maker must aim to reproduce their life in others.

Second, Jesus expected his disciples to observe his works. Disciple-making can be done by the pastors as they set an example for their flock to follow, just like what Paul did with the churches he started. Yet the importance of a more personal and intentional approach to disciple-making should not be ignored. Disciple-making can be done one-on-one, but we have enough evidence from Scripture that one-on-one discipleship is not the only right way to do it. Jesus had twelve. Nonetheless, we cannot ignore the fact that there is no way a pastor can disciple every member of the congregation, especially as the community continues to grow in size. However, the fact that pastors cannot disciple everyone does not mean they cannot disciple a few who can reproduce their lives in others. Jesus did not disciple the crowd; but he chose only twelve "so that they would be with Him and that He could send them out to preach, and to have authority to cast out the demons" (Mark 3:14–15). In other words, while many believe in Jesus, who, for sure were touched by Jesus's life and message, and were willing to imitate him, Jesus still chose to invest his life on twelve so they can be close enough to him to observe his life, and to continue the work he had done.

Third, Jesus wanted them to understand his vision. The Great Commission is the clearest expression of Jesus's vision for discipleship. Even before Jesus's death and resurrection, he had already been informing his disciples that he expected them to do the same things he did, whether it be the "works" or miracles he performed (John 14:12), or the sufferings he went through (Matt 10:23–24), or the message he proclaimed (10:7). Before the ascension, he made clear that he wanted them to make disciples the way he did. The pastors as disciple-maker must also instill this vision in the mind of the congregation. In this generation, the pulpit seems to be one of the best way to do so. Ogden observes,

> Preachers in disciple-making churches need to see themselves as more than careful expositors of God's Word, as important as that is. They are the vision casters for disciple making, which is backed up with their life investments as personal disciple

makers. They lead the disciple-making strategy and view preaching as one significant component in this process.[6]

Fourth, Jesus wanted them to do the same. Jesus instructed his disciples that in the same way he trained them to become disciples by "teaching them to obey" the commands of God, he wanted them to do the same.

Nurture

Making disciples of all nations involves three elements: going, baptizing, and teaching. "Going" involves the work of evangelism and "baptizing" is the process of incorporating the new believers into the believing community. We will discuss more about these two in the chapter on *The Pastor as an Evangelist/Apologist*. The period between the first instance a person hears the gospel and the time the person makes a commitment to follow Christ and be baptized varies from individual to individual. Some may take shorter time before they make the decision while others take longer; likewise, the third stage of disciple-making may vary in length of time. What is clear is the goal to which we want to bring these disciples—a life of obedience. Jesus commanded his disciples to make other disciples by "teaching them to obey," which is part of a person's continuous transformation to becoming more like Jesus.

Transformation usually happens incrementally, and it happens best in the context of a community whose members share the same goal of becoming more like Christ. Ogden shares his observation based on his personal experience.

> I contend that a necessary and pivotal element in providing the motivation and discipline to grow self-initiating, reproducing, fully devoted followers of Jesus comes only through personal investment. The motivation and discipline will not ultimately occur through listening to sermons, sitting in a class, participating in a fellowship group, attending a study group in the workplace or being a member of a small group, but rather in the context of highly accountable, relationally transparent, truth-centered, small (three or four people) discipleship units. In my experience this is the optimum context for transformation.[7]

Transformations begins with the commitment to obedience. Jesus taught many things about obedience. First, he reminded his disciples that

6. Ogden, *Transforming Discipleship*, 198.
7. Ogden, *Transforming Discipleship*, 56.

obedience to his commands would not be easy, and that at times, may even result in various forms of persecution. We do not find this being discussed in many of the works about discipleship. The primary reason, it seems, is that very few writers come from places where there is real persecution. However, for many followers of Jesus even in this era, obedience can be costly. Thus, it is important for his followers to be ready and stand their ground when persecutions come. Jesus warned his followers about the different kinds of persecution. Believers may be hated and slandered, sometimes even by their own family, because they do not share the values and beliefs of the people around them (Matt 10:16–25). The cost of discipleship is high that obedience to Jesus may at times endanger their lives (16:24–28). Jesus encouraged his followers by reminding them, "Blessed are those who are persecuted for righteousness' sake, for theirs is the kingdom of heaven" (5:10).

Second, Jesus explained that the pursuit of righteousness is the essence of obedience. Jesus redefined "righteousness" by showing his disciples that it is more than an outward performance. There is more to righteousness than meeting the demands of the written Law. Understanding the essential principles behind the Law and applying it in comparable situations is necessary. The principle Jesus taught his disciples is not new. After God gave the Ten Commandments through Moses (Exod 20:1–22), for example, he followed it up with a series of commandments that provide various instances wherein these ten commands can be applied. God did not just prohibit the worship of other gods and the making of idols, but also prescribed ways for Israel to properly worship him (20:22–26). God did not just command them to honor the Sabbath, but gave commands on how to properly treat slaves by allowing them to have Sabbath (21:1–11). God did not just command them to honor their parents, but provided examples how to do so through words (Lev 20:9) or deeds (20:11). God did not just prohibit murder, but he also taught them to value life (Exod 21:12–32). God did not just prohibit adultery, but taught the people to distinguish between proper and improper sexual practices (Lev 20:10–21). God did not just prohibit stealing, but taught the people to respect the properties of their neighbors (Exod 22:1–15). God did not just prohibit the giving of false witnesses, but commanded the people to promote justice (23:1–9). God did not just prohibit covetousness, but also warned them how people can fall into its trap (Deut 7:25). Jesus elaborated on the essence of the Law in his Sermon on the Mount.

Third, Jesus also taught his followers that righteousness must not be pursued for self-glorification (Matt 6:1–2, 5, 16). Thus, Jesus warned against practicing the spiritual disciplines like almsgiving, prayer, and fasting for the purpose of showing off. This is the reason for the confrontations between Jesus and the religious leaders of his generation.

THE PASTOR AS A DISCIPLE-MAKER

Jesus's final command to his disciples prior to his ascension was to make disciples of all nations. It is practically impossible for a pastor to single-handedly disciple everyone in the congregation. This is why pastors need to train others to do so. Training others to make disciple is an essential part of discipleship. We will discuss more about training in the next chapter *The Pastor as a Teacher/Trainer*. In this chapter, we focused on another essential element of disciple-making, and that is teaching others to obey.

Disciple-making pastors teach others to obey, and as they teach, they must LEARN.

- Listen: Disciple-makers listen to God and obey him before teaching others to obey.
- Explain: The Scripture is the unchanging basis of our teaching, and the pastors must explain it to their disciples.
- Admonish: Using the principles from the Bible, disciple-making pastors must admonish their disciples to encourage proper behaviors and correct the wrong ones.
- Reproduce: Disciple-makers also train others to reproduce their life in others.
- Nurture: Disciple-makers nurture their disciples understanding that the goal of discipleship is transformation.

Questions for Personal Reflection

Listen: How is your personal walk with God? Is there anything in your life that prevents you from listening to God openly and wholeheartedly?

Explain: How can you make sure that you consistently grow in you understanding of the Scripture? What specific steps can you take to ensure this?

Admonish: If you are discipling members of your congregation, how can you encourage them to continue living consistently according to the Scripture's teachings? Have you established good relationship with them so that you are able to correct them if necessary? As a pastor, are you willing to receive corrections from them if necessary?

Reproduce: How do you encourage members to make disciples also? Do you set an example for them to follow? Do you provide trainings for those who wanted to do so?

Nurture: How do you encourage openness and mutual accountability with your disciples? How do you help them gauge whether they are experiencing transformation in their life so as to become more like Jesus?

5

The Pastor as a Teacher/Trainer

The Lord's call to every believer is to serve Him and others. Every believer has gifts by the Lord to enhance the work of the church. Human nature's call, however, is to personal convenience and personal comfort. The pastor-teacher lives in the gulf between the Lord's will and individual human wills in the church. He calls out the called and equips them to use their gifts effectively.[1]

—RICK YOUNT

MARK TELLS THE STORY about the inability of the disciples to heal the boy with an unclean spirit (9:14–29). In Jesus's absence, the people brought the boy to his disciples expecting them to heal him, but they were unable to do so. When Jesus came, he reprimanded his disciples, not for attempting to imitate his works, but for lacking faith (9:19). His statement shows that he wanted and expected his disciples to do what he was doing. It also presumes that they were previously instructed to continue his ministry and do the work he was doing.

Matthew and Luke also recount the time when Jesus sent out his disciples to proclaim his teachings (Matt 10:5–8; Luke 9:1–2). He did this long before his ascension, before which he instructed them for the last time to

---

1. Yount, "The Pastor as Teacher," 170.

continue in their work of proclaiming God's kingdom (Mark 16:15-18). In other words, within the short period Jesus was with his disciples, he did not just teach them lessons about character, but he also provided them training so that they can continue doing his work.

The number people who are *willing* to serve in churches are often more than the number of people who are *actually* serving; and often, many who desired to serve hesitate because they feel they lack the training to serve effectively. One of the essential roles of the pastor is to teach and train his flock so they can be involved in God's work as well. As the teacher/trainer, the pastors must TEACH: Train their congregation by assigning work to them, Equip them with the goal of building the body of Christ, Affirm those who serve faithfully, Commission them to do specific tasks, and Hope for the best for every worker.

TEACHERS/TRAINERS TEACH

Train

Much like driving a car and swimming, ministry is best learned by doing it. This is true for both pastors and lay ministers. This means that one of the responsibilities of the pastor as a teacher/trainer is to open and provide opportunities for the people to minister. One method of doing so is delegation.

Jethro's advice to Moses typically comes to mind whenever the topic of delegation is discussed. Exodus 12:37 tells us that there were six hundred thousand men who came out from Egypt with Moses; together with the women and children, the total number of people with Moses could be somewhere between one-and-a-half to two million. As the leader and judge of the people, Moses would make decisions for them every day from morning until evening (18:13). This practice did not only wear out Moses, but also the people standing in line waiting for their concerns to be heard and a decision about them be made (18:18). Thus, Jethro advised Moses to do two things: (1) teach the people God's statutes (18:19-20), so that they would be able to make decisions for themselves based on God's teachings; and (2) appoint men with both character and ability from among the Israelites who would be able to do many of the things Moses was doing (18:21-22).

There are three parties involved here: Moses the delegator, the congregation, and the appointed delegatees. Jethro's advice was not only good for Moses the delegator and congregation because the system kept them from unnecessarily wearing out, but it also provided many people the opportunity to serve like Moses, which became beneficial for the congregation. One of the clearest benefits of delegating is that it keeps the delegator from burning out. The pastor as teacher/trainer must understand, however, that *avoiding burnout should not be the only motivation for delegating tasks to others*. Delegation is an essential part of training people. Even Jethro understood this principle, "Moreover, look for able men from all the people, men who fear God, who are trustworthy and hate a bribe, and place such men over the people as chiefs of thousands, of hundreds, of fifties, and of tens. And *let them judge the people at all times*. Every great matter they shall bring to you, but any small matter they shall decide themselves. So it will be easier for you, and *they will bear the burden with you*" (18:21–22, italics added). Jethro's words, "let them judge the people at all times," suggests that some people are expected to do Moses's work. Moreover, Jethro said, "they will bear the burden with you"; he did not say, "so that you will be relieved of the burden." Delegation is more about empowering people rather than lessening the leader's workload. When we assign task to others only because we are overwhelmed with our work, we are not delegating, we are just avoiding the pressures we do not want to handle. Real delegation is the willingness to give opportunities to others so they can serve God together with us; it is assigning tasks to them *even if we can do the task alone*, knowing that the only way for them to have a firsthand learning is when we give them the opportunity to experience doing the work.

Moses's willingness to delegate is commendable for several reasons. First, it shows that he acknowledged his personal limitations—that as an individual he cannot do everything by himself. This explains Moses's words to the Israelites just before they entered the Land, "How can I bear by myself the weight and burden of you and your strife? Choose for your tribes wise, understanding, and experienced men, and I will appoint them as your heads" (Deut 1:12–13). Second, it shows his real motive for serving—that it was not for the purpose of making himself the center of everything. This explains why Moses did not find it necessary to defend himself when his own siblings were questioning his authority (Num 12:1–16). Third, it shows that he trusts God's work in the lives of others—that in the same way God worked through him, God can do so through others. This also explains why Moses, when asked by Joshua to stop Eldad and Medad from prophesying, replied, "Are you jealous for my sake? Would that all the LORD's people were prophets, that the LORD would put his Spirit on them!" (11:29).

Delegation can be risky because we do not know whether the person will be responsible and faithful in doing the work. This is the reason we must be clear about the qualities that we are looking for from a person to whom we delegate a task. Jethro gave his suggestion for those who would be serving as judges, "look for able men from all the people, men who fear

God, who are trustworthy and hate a bribe" (Exod 18:21). Likewise, the pastor as teacher/trainer has a responsibility to make sure the people to whom they delegate a task meet certain character requirements.

Equip

In writing to the Ephesians, Paul cites unity as one of the important goals for which the church should aim. He explains that the church is one body, having one Spirit, sharing one hope, subject to only one Lord, holding on to one faith, acknowledging one baptism, and have come from one God and Father (Eph 4:4–6). With everything we share in common, unity is already a given, but it can fully be experienced only if the members do their part to contribute to its fulfillment. Every member must do their part to contribute to the building up of the body of Christ, whether through good interpersonal relationships (4:25–32) or through serving in various capacities (4:12–13). Pastors need to constantly remind the church about the importance of good interpersonal relationships. The body of Christ is built up through mutual encouragements and truthful speech. Moreover, pastors have the responsibility, not only to constantly remind the congregation that they should be involved in God's work, but also to equip members to serve, making sure that the member's gifts are developed and maximized.

Just like the physical body which is composed of different parts performing different functions, the church is also composed of various parts expected to perform various duties and each part dependent upon God's Spirit. Paul explains, "Now there are varieties of gifts, but the same Spirit; and there are varieties of service, but the same Lord; and there are varieties of activities, but it is *the same God who empowers them all in everyone.* To each is given the manifestation of the Spirit for the common good" (1 Cor 12:4–7, italics added). The pastors as teacher/trainer need to take responsibility in training the members for ministry, yet they must consider the various gifts of the members of the congregation and remember that ultimately, it is the Spirit's task to prepare every believer for ministry. Ron Dalton summarizes the work of the Spirit:

> The cleansing, empowering, and equipping work of the Holy Spirit provides the body of Christ what is needed to be faithful to God's calling. It needs to be emphasized that Paul's understanding of the spiritual gifts encompasses the whole body and not just the leaders. No one is expected to have all of these

spiritual gifts. No one is excluded from being a potential means through whom the Spirit might work.[2]

Just like the physical body, although different parts have different functions, we do not consider one as more important than the others. So also, in the church, while members have different functions, one need not be considered more important than others (1 Cor 12:12–25). The body of Christ is built when members perform their respective tasks; and this can happen only if the pastors take the responsibility of training the members to serve.

An important reminder: even pastors are gifted differently, and therefore they cannot be expected to have the ability to provide *all kinds* of ministry training. Although the pastors cannot provide all kinds of training, they can initiate, facilitate, and coordinate various trainings for the congregation. On some occasions, short seminars or workshops that provide the members practical tips on how to perform particular ministries are enough to get them involved. They can also create opportunities, encourage, and challenge people to serve because the best way to learn how to do ministry is a firsthand and on-the-job experience. All these with the *sole purpose* of building up the body of Christ.

While we must acknowledge the uniqueness of every member of the body of Christ, we must not lose sight of what we have in common. As Dalton reminds us,

> Whether we're preachers, pastors, administrators, teachers, evangelists, missionaries, compassionate ministry workers, clergy, or laypersons, full- or part-time, paid or volunteer, we join our uniqueness with others and engage our shared stories of salvation, calling, and gifting. In joining our lives together as the body of Christ, we come to help, encourage, and learn from each other. We share within this spiritual ministerial fellowship much of the same fears, challenges, and values. We are all unique, but we are also more alike than we often realize.[3]

The purpose of celebrating our uniqueness is to promote unity. Unity can be achieved if the leaders take responsibility in training the members to serve in various areas of ministry. Paul describes the duty of the church leaders: "to equip the saints for the work of ministry, for building up the body of Christ, *until we all attain to the unity* of the faith and of the knowledge of the Son of God, to mature manhood, to the measure of the stature of

---

2. Dalton, *Discovering Christian Ministry*, 88.
3. Dalton, *Discovering Christian Ministry*, 96.

the fullness of Christ" (Eph 4:12–13, italics added). The goal is unity, which is the ultimate gauge of maturity and Christlikeness; the means is having members serve in various capacities which can happen only if the pastors make the effort to equip.

Affirm

As a teacher/trainer, pastors (especially those with administrative responsibilities) must learn how to place the right people in the right ministries. Again, it is important to note that putting the right person in the right place is to be done with the *sole purpose* of building up the body of Christ. The temptation of placing certain people in certain positions to advance one's personal agenda is real. Pastors are not exempt from this kind of temptation, and even pastors sometimes succumb to it. Assigning the right person to the right task is a way for the pastors to affirm the individual strength of the members of the congregation.

Giving the right people the right task is also a way to acknowledge that spiritual gifts and abilities come from one source, and doing so is a way to honor God and acknowledge his work among us. After the Israelites came out from Egypt, as they were preparing to enter the Land, God instructed them to build the Tabernacle. Some Israelites, out of generosity, contributed materials for the work (Exod 35:5, 21); thus, everyone who possessed the needed materials brought their material contributions (35:22–24). Others offered their skills and did some work (35:25–26); and there were others, like Bezalel and Oholiab, who not only offered themselves do the work, but were also inspired to teach others to do the work (35:34).

Even in the building of the temple, workers were tasked to do work according to their skills. The Tyrian bronze smith, Hiram, was appointed to do all bronze work (1 Kgs 7:14); stonecutters, masons, and carpenters were assigned to work according to their skills (1 Chr 22:15). After its completion, people were trained to perform their tasks and workers are assigned tasks according to their skills. The singers in the temple were trained to develop their skills in singing (1 Chr 25:7), and the same was expected of the musicians (2 Chr 34:12); even the priests and Levites were trained to perform their duties skillfully (2:7; 30:22); Huram-abi was tasked to do the engravings and work with fabrics according to his skill (2:13–14); and there were machines used in the temple invented by skilled men (26:15).

In these two accounts, there are two kinds of people: those who give material goods; and those who use their time and skills to do the work. There is one important principle that we must remember: *Those who bring material contributions are not more important than those who contribute their skills, nor are those who offer their time and work better than those who offer material possessions.* In many contexts, those who give material offerings (the donors, the "big" tithers, the "financiers") are often given more honor than those who are working in the field. Almost all kinds of ministries need funds, and the lack of funds are often the reason some ministries are stalled, hence, the honor given to the donors, which is good unless it causes the church to operate under the financial Golden Rule, "Whoever has the Gold, makes the Rules." Similarly, those who are involved in ministries that are visible receive greater affirmation than those behind the scenes. Ministries that are less visible are often taken for granted as if tasks were accomplished by themselves. The pastor as the teacher/trainer has the responsibility to educate the congregation and constantly remind them that every contribution is important, whether it be material possessions or skills. The principle of the body is also applicable here. In the same way that the members of the body, albeit diverse, are part of one body, so also the members of believing congregation, regardless of their various skills and contribution, are part of one body and are equally important. Moreover, the contributions of these members, whether it be material possession or skilled work, are also equally important as long as they are given with the *sole purpose* of building up the body of Christ.

During the time of Hezekiah, he led the celebration of the Passover and one of the highlights of the celebration is the honoring of those who use their skills to serve God faithfully, "And Hezekiah *spoke encouragingly to all the Levites who showed good skill in the service of the* Lord. So they ate the food of the festival for seven days, sacrificing peace offerings and giving thanks to the Lord, the God of their fathers" (2 Chr 30.22, italics added). People have skills only because the Lord has given them the skill (e.g., Exod 36:1); and the pastor, as a teacher/trainer, can affirm the Lord's work by placing the right people in the right ministry.

Commission

The fact that "equipping the saints" is included in the pastor's job description is enough to show that God never intended church ministry to be a one-man-show. There may be circumstances that force the pastors to do so, but Paul's description of the pastor's task suggests that this should not be the norm. Thus, pastors should include in his ministry plans to train workers who can serve in different ministries, and when these workers are ready, to commission them to perform their respective tasks.

Paul wrote two personal letters to Timothy and one to Titus; both were pastors of churches Paul and his team pioneered. Both pastors were also assigned by Paul to shepherd the congregations in Ephesus and Crete. Paul commanded Titus, "This is why I left you in Crete, so that you might put what remained into order, and appoint elders in every town as I directed you" (Tit 1:5). Paul envisioned local churches, not only to produce lay ministers who can serve, but also to have people who can be trained to be elders/pastors and deacons. Thus, Paul presented to Timothy and Titus a list of qualities they should look for in people they would appoint as elders/pastors and deacons. The list of qualifications for elders and deacons may not be exactly the same, but they are comparable. Three major qualities are expected. First, they should be people of integrity; this must be seen in various areas of their life including their marriage, the way they handle finances, their speech, among others. Second, they are expected to be faithful to the Word; whether it means the ability to teach (1 Tim 3:2) or faithfulness in holding to the teachings of the Scripture (3:9; Tit 1:9). Third, even their reputation among unbelievers is also important (1 Tim 3:7). Having met these basic qualifications, they can be commissioned to function as elders/pastors or deacons.

We have earlier discussed the need to delegate tasks to others because it is part of training others. Delegation is a way to affirm the priesthood of all believers and God's vision for the ministry which is the participation of every member in his service. Below is an excerpt from the work of Derek J. Prime and Alistair Begg that seems worth quoting at length:

> Delegation is an essential extension of effective leadership, and it demands separate consideration. Leadership may be defined as the ability to give rise to other leaders, but it is also the ability to develop other people's maximum potential for their own works of service in the body of Christ. This goal can be achieved only through delegation. The title "overseers" given to the shepherds and teachers implies that we are to superintend certain tasks rather than to accomplish them ourselves. The qualification for elders that they should be able to teach (1 Timothy 3:2) may include not only the ability to teach Christian doctrine and conduct, but also the passing on of information and skills so that people achieve the works of service God has foreordained for them.
>
> Delegation is part of our public recognition that the ministry is that of the whole church. While we have high views of our calling as shepherds and teachers—or "ministers" as we will often be called—the unhelpful concepts of "clergy" and "laity"

should be discarded. This way of thinking has focused so many aspects of ministry upon one individual, creating a "one-man ministry." Too many things tend to be expected of the conventional pastor. One means of avoiding this snare is a proper emphasis upon shared leadership, and establishing that "the minister" is but an elder among elders, although called to be a "presiding elder."[4]

Pastors must not only aim to reproduce their life in others (as disciple-maker), but also to train others to serve. Pastors must not only aim to train the congregation for service, but also (and especially) those who are called to serve as pastors. Pastors can train future pastors by giving opportunities for them to serve in various ministries; keeping in mind that seminary training remains essential in training new pastors. There are certain types of training that only seminaries can provide. The habit of rigorous study, for instance, is best acquired in an environment provided by seminaries. There are also certain types of training that is best learned through actual involvement in ministries of local churches, such as doing outreaches, ministering to various age groups, among others. Pastors must be involved in training new pastors who can serve alongside them.

Hope

Training people to serve in churches is one of the important responsibilities of the pastor. It is both rewarding and risky. It is rewarding because nothing can replace a trainer's joy in seeing his trainees meet or even exceed expectations, and be able to accomplish more than what the trainer can do or have done. Even Jesus envisioned his disciples doing "greater works" than what he had done (John 14:12). Clearly, some of the works Jesus accomplished can never be duplicated by any of his followers, but he expected them to accomplish "greater works" in the sense that the extent to which the Gospel had reached through his disciples is broader than what Jesus had reached during his earthly ministry, and the number of people who heard the message through the succeeding generations of disciples is more than those who personally heard Jesus. Likewise, Paul expressed his joy, not only because of seeing faithful people like Eunice and Lois train their children to be godly, but also for seeing the younger believers mature and become ready to serve God (2 Tim 1:4–7).

Faithfully training others to serve does not always guarantee good results. Paul knew the pain of seeing coworkers discontinue serving God for

---

4. Prime and Begg, *On Being a Pastor*, 224–25.

various reasons. Demas, for instance, was one of Paul's missionary companions (Col 4:14; Phlm 24). He later deserted Paul because, as Paul assessed, he "loved the present world" (2 Tim 4:10). Demas might have reached the point when he felt that following Christ is too costly and he was no longer willing to continue carrying his cross, and so he deserted the team; or perhaps he could not resist the temptations of fame or fortune. Regardless of his reason for leaving the ministry, it shows the risks every pastor must take as they train coworkers to serve with them.

Another coworker of Paul withdrew from their mission for reasons not mentioned in the story (Acts 15:36–40). When Paul and Barnabas wanted to visit the believers in Asia Minor again, Barnabas wanted to bring Mark while Paul did not want to do so because Mark withdrew from their earlier mission (15:38). Whatever Mark's reason for leaving, his lack of perseverance resulted in a rift between Paul and Barnabas (15:39–40).

The New Testament does not tell us whether Demas was later restored, but as for Mark, there are indications that the once half-hearted coworker eventually turned out to be one of Paul's faithful coworkers. Mark ministered alongside the members of Paul's mission team (Col 4:7–14; Phlm 23–25); and Paul openly commended him for his faithfulness (2 Tim 4:11). Barnabas's willingness to give Mark another chance might be one of the factors that helped Mark get back on track. The book of Acts shows us that Barnabas was willing to take risks on people even though many others have doubts. Luke tells us that he took the risk for Paul (Acts 9:26–27); he also did the same to Mark (15:36–40). The risks Barnabas took gave Paul the opportunity to turn from a zealous persecutor of Christians to become a persecuted Christian, from a murderer who was not afraid to kill followers of Christ to a martyr who was not afraid to die for following Christ. Likewise, the risks Barnabas took with Mark helped him to turn from a half-hearted missionary to a faithful servant "useful for the ministry."

Training people is a risk because some may not turn out well, but pastors can always trust God's work in the life of our trainees. As pastors choose their trainees wisely, with proper encouragements and timely instructions, we can hope for the best in our trainees. Nonetheless, knowing that they are imperfect people like us, we need to allow them to make mistakes and learn from it, hoping for God's work in their life. We need to learn to see them, not for what they already are, but for what they can become.

THE PASTOR AS A TEACHER/TRAINER

Paul's view about the reason God raised up people to assume different leadership roles is clear, "to equip the saints for the work of ministry, for building up the body of Christ, until we all attain to the unity of the faith and of the knowledge of the Son of God, to mature manhood, to the measure of the stature of the fullness of Christ" (Eph 4:12–13). Pastors are called, not to perform in a one-man-show, but to equip the believers in order that they can get involved in the work; to delegate, not primarily to avoid stress in the ministry, but to train God's people because God intended every member of the congregation to be part of his work. This is God's design for building the body of Christ—to attain unity in the body of Christ by getting the people involved in God's work.

The pastor's role as a teacher/trainer is to equip the members so they can serve in various ministries. To do so, the pastors must TEACH.

- Train: Train them by giving opportunities for them to serve.
- Equip: Provide different kinds of training for them because every member is gifted differently.
- Affirm: Acknowledge the various contributions of the members of the congregation because no one contribution is more important than the others.
- Commission: Delegation is not giving to others the work we do not like, but allowing others to flourish in their area of giftedness.
- Hope: Knowing that every member has strengths and weaknesses, we acknowledge that only God can work in the lives of the members so that they can improve in their service.

Questions for Personal Reflection

Train: What are some of the work that you can start delegating to others? What is the reason that you want to delegate these tasks? Is it because you do not like to do them or because it is part of training the members?

Equip: Considering the members of your congregation, what sort of training do they need? Are you able to provide these training for them? If so, how do you plan to train them for service? If you are unable to provide the training they need, how can you facilitate the training for them?

Affirm: How can you affirm the various contributions of the members of the congregation? How can you encourage them so that they can continue serving God?

Commission: As a pastor or leader, is there any reason that keeps you from delegating tasks to others? Is it because the coworkers are not reliable? Is it for fear that they will do a better job?

Hope: Do you have coworkers who are like Demas or Mark? How can you be a Barnabas to them? How can you help them change their attitude toward God's work?

6

The Pastor as an Exegete/Prophet

The pastor is the inheritor of the privilege and responsibility of leading the people of God, specifically, via the new-covenant ministry of reconciliation . . . this divine appointment too requires pastors—like prophets, priests, and kings before them—to speak God's Word to God's people, intercede to God on their behalf, and model the wisdom of salvation life.[1]

—Kevin J. Vanhoozer and Owen Strachan

Prophets are often regarded as people whose ministry is to foretell the future. This is correct, but only partially. Many of them proclaimed messages they received as direct revelation from God; these messages include the specifics like the time of judgment and the nations involved, the type of calamity or blessing that can be anticipated. However, we must not ignore the fact that prophets were preachers who proclaimed God's message on the basis of the Law given to Moses.

Even in Daniel's prayer, he acknowledged, "All Israel has transgressed your law and turned aside, refusing to obey your voice. And the curse and oath that are *written in the Law of Moses* the servant of God have been poured out upon us, because we have sinned against him . . . As it is *written*

---

1. Vanhoozer and Strachan, *The Pastor as Public Theologian*, 39.

in the Law of Moses, all this calamity has come upon us" (Dan 9:11, 13; italics added). God also spoke through Malachi, "Remember the *law of my servant Moses*, the statutes and rules that I commanded him at Horeb for all Israel" (Mal 4:4, italics added). In short, prophets were preachers who based their messages from the Law.

The prophet's task, therefore, is to interpret God's word and preach his message on the basis of the Scripture available to them, which is the Law of Moses. In this sense, the work of the pastor is much like the work of a prophet—preach God's word based on the Scripture. This is the reason it is important for pastors to carefully interpret the Word. Exegesis and prophecy are inseparable. As an exegete and prophet, the pastors must SPEAK: preach with the Scripture as the sole basis of authority for life and doctrines, Persevere regardless of the people's response, Exhort to build up the body of Christ, aim for Accuracy of contents, and Kneel before God who is the source of power for preaching.

EXEGETES/PROPHETS SPEAK

Scripture

The Scripture is the sole basis for preaching. In it is the essential message that we proclaim. Although we must recognize that truths can be found in many sources (e.g., scientific facts, history); but when it comes to the Christian's life and beliefs, the Bible is our sole authority. Prime and Begg remind us,

> Preaching, like other good gifts of God, has been abused. Some have used the pulpit as a coward's castle from which they made pronouncements without having to take public criticism in return. They have used it to forward their own ideas rather than gospel truth. But our concern is with the preaching of God's Word, not the propagation of human ideas or opinions.[2]

Jesus set an example for us to follow. While attending a regular Sabbath meeting at a local synagogue in Nazareth, when it was his turn to read the Scripture, Jesus took the opportunity not just to read the Scripture, but also to explain it to those who were present (Luke 4:17–21). After reading Isaiah 61:1–2, he claimed, "Today this Scripture has been fulfilled in your hearing" (Luke 4:21). In the same way, after his resurrection, while walking to Emmaus with two of his followers who were unable to recognize him, he explained the purpose of the Messiah's death, and "beginning with Moses

2. Prime and Begg, *On Being a Pastor*, 118.

and all the Prophets, he interpreted to them in all the Scriptures the things concerning himself" (24:27). He did the same when he appeared to his disciples. He opened their minds to understand the prophecies, explaining these prophecies to them (24:44–47).

Jesus's disciples followed their teacher's example. The Scripture was central to the decision-making and preaching of the apostles. The apostles had the Scripture as their basis in deciding to add another disciple of Jesus to their group. Peter used the Scripture to explain how they should find a replacement for Judas (Acts 1:16). When the Spirit came upon the believers at Pentecost and they spoke in different languages, Peter appealed to Scripture to explain the incident as the fulfillment of Joel's prophecy (2:16–20; cf. Joel 2:28–32). From this, Peter preach his first recorded sermon, explaining the events in the life of Jesus in light of the psalms and the prophets (Acts 2:14–36). Peter preached another sermon at Solomon's portico (3:12–26), pointing the listeners to God's promise to Moses (3:22–23; see also Deut 18:18).

Both Stephen (Acts 7:2–53) and Paul (15:16–41) preached by summarizing the works of God in Israel, and for both of them, the words of Moses (7:37; 13:15) and the prophets (7:42, 48, 52; 13:15, 27, 40) were the basis for their message. Philip also preached on the basis of Isaiah 53 (cf. Acts 8:30–35); he "opened his mouth, and beginning with this Scripture he told him the good news about Jesus" (8:35). Paul brought the same message and preached from the same Scripture even to the Jews in the Diaspora and to the Gentiles (17:2). While speaking to the Jews in Rome, "From morning till evening [Paul] expounded to them, testifying to the kingdom of God and trying to convince them about Jesus both *from the Law of Moses and from the Prophets*" (28:23, italics added).

If we are convinced that the Scripture is God's word and that it includes both the Old and the New Testaments, pastors as exegete/prophet must carefully interpret and preach from both the Old and New Testaments, not just our favorite portions of it. Let us not forget that over three-fourths (actually, close to four-fifths) of the Bible is the Old Testament, and if we only preach from the New Testament, we are missing a significant portion of the Bible. That is why it is important to make sure our congregation receives a balanced feeding from both testaments. This requires a conscious effort on the part of the pastor to plan their preaching schedule so that the congregation receives enough feeding from both testaments.

Consecutive expository preaching has its advantages and there are many reasons it is a good practice. A word of caution is needed, however; pastors should be careful not to fall into the temptation of thinking that expository preaching is *the only correct way* to preach, or doing it consecutively is always better. One thing we can be sure of, there is not a shred of evidence that Jesus was an expository preacher the way we define it today. To insist that it is the only right way of preaching is nothing short of arrogance. The most important thing is faithful interpretation of the Scripture, and boldly proclaiming its message even if it may be offensive to some listeners. This leads us to the second task of the pastor as an exegete/prophet—to persevere.

Persevere

There are several reasons why preaching can be challenging. First, the preparation can be tedious. For those who are new in this ministry, it may take twenty or even thirty hours just to prepare a 20- to 30-minute sermon. Even for those who had already been preaching for some time, it may take as much as 15 hours of preparation to write one sermon. Choosing the right passage and appropriate illustrations can also pose as a challenge. Since preaching is not a presentation of our exegetical notes, we need to "put flesh" on these notes to help the congregation understand the passage so that they do not only know what the text teaches, but also how to apply these teachings; and this is more challenging than just knowing what the text says.

Second, the task of preaching can be difficult. For most preachers, it takes a while to get comfortable speaking publicly and develop a personal style in delivering a message. An additional pressure is the congregation's expectations, which may be unrealistic at times. The preacher must strive to constantly improve in both preparation and delivery of the message. These are the only areas preachers can control. The message is not negotiable, and sometimes the message itself can be offensive (we shall discuss more about this later). Preachers need to remember, however, that the fact that the message is offensive does not mean that we must *intend* to offend people and that the *manner of delivery* must be offensive. There are ways to proclaim offensive messages *tactfully, discreetly, and respectfully*. In preaching, *recklessness in speech is not equivalent to faithfulness to the word*. They are two different things. Let us not confuse the manner of delivery with the contents of the message. The contents may be offensive, the manner of delivery need not be. It all boils down to the preacher's attitude. Many preachers confuse the two so they have no qualms using sarcasms, belittling other religious groups, and berating even Christians who do not share their views on certain issues. The only part that should be offensive is the message and not the manner of delivery. This leads us to the third difficulty: the offensive nature of the Gospel message.

Third, the message we must preach may not always be pleasant to hear. The people's response varies: most members welcome both encouragement and rebuke, some accept only things that are pleasant to the ears, but there are those who may still listen but reject most of what the pastor says. The Bible's message is not always encouraging; it can sometimes be offensive which makes it difficult both for the preacher and the listener. At times, preachers may feel uncomfortable preaching certain passages because of this. As mentioned earlier (but it is worth repeating again), the only thing that should be offensive is the message and not the manner of delivery. There are similarities between preaching and raising children—we do not have to use insults and derogatory language or be abusive in speech to get the message across. We do not have to intentionally offend people; we just have to faithfully preach the message. The fact that God had to encourage some prophets to preach offensive messages despite the people's response shows that it was not their *intention* to offend the people with their message. Ezekiel, for instance, was called by God to preach with these instructions and warnings, "And you, son of man, be not afraid of them, nor be afraid of their words, though briers and thorns are with you and you sit on scorpions. Be not afraid of their words, nor be dismayed at their looks, for they are a rebellious house. And you shall speak my words to them, whether they hear or refuse to hear, for they are a rebellious house" (Ezek 2:6–7). The response of the listeners was not the reason he should stop preaching. Likewise, preachers today should not preach only because people like to listen; preachers should preach because God called them to preach, even if there are some who refuse to listen. If it is God who calls the preacher to preach, and only God can tell the preacher to stop preaching.

Fourth, the listeners may not always respond positively. Even in churches, there are those who come to the service, not with a sermon notebook, but with an evaluation form. Preachers have no control of the people's response. Therefore, preachers need to learn perseverance as they preach. If there are preachers who confuse the lack of tact in preaching with faithfulness to the word, there are also members of the congregation who confuse having a critical spirit with being like the Bereans. Just like God's warning to Ezekiel, preachers must preach even if there are people who refuse to listen. Similarly, Paul's instruction to Timothy was to "preach the word; be ready in season and out of season; reprove, rebuke, and exhort, with complete patience and teaching" (2 Tim 4:2). Earlier, he told Timothy to "fan into flame the gift of God" (1:6). Verse 8 tells us the gift is related to preaching, "Therefore do not be ashamed of the testimony about our Lord" (1:8a). Paul's command to preach the word in season and out of season came with an acknowledgement that God called and gifted Timothy to preach and that God has given him a spirit of "power and love and self-control" (1:7). As a preacher, he must preach with "power" and proclaim the message with boldness regardless of the people's response; he must also preach with "love" and speak with humility so that only the message is "offensive," not the preacher's attitude and manner of delivery; and he must preach with "self-control" and speak *only* the message of God.

Exhort

As discussed earlier, the message of the Scripture is *inevitably* offensive at times; thus, the messenger must be bold to preach the message even if there are people who will refuse to listen. However, the Gospel *is* good news; thus, the preacher must proclaim the message of Scripture as such. Jesus was clear about his goal in ministry (Luke 4:18-19). In the process, he had to confront the sins of humanity and the evils in the society; but this does not nullify the fact that he preached good news.

It is one thing to preach an offensive message *out of necessity*, it is another thing to *make it our pursuit*. Why? Because a sermon is basically a word of exhortation. While Paul and Barnabas were at Antioch of Pisidia, they attended a Sabbath meeting in the local synagogue. Luke tells us that after the Scripture was read, the presider said, "Brothers, if you have any *word of encouragement* for the people, say it" (Acts 13:15, italics added). After which, Paul stood up and preached a sermon (13:16-41). What is one important takeaway from this incident? A sermon is a "word of encouragement." In the New Testament, we do not only have short sermons like that of Paul in Acts 13, we even have a full sermon manuscript like the book of Hebrews. This is what the author of Hebrews claimed to have written, "I appeal to you, brothers, bear with my *word of exhortation*, for I have written to you briefly" (Heb 13:22, italics added).

The "word of encouragement" in the New Testament can include a lot of things. First, it includes a review of how God worked in the past (Acts 13:16-23; Heb 1:1-2). God's work in the past is an invitation for us to believe in him at present because this same God is still at work today. Second, the "word of exhortation" is a call to repentance (Acts 13:24-25) and an announcement of God's forgiveness (Acts 13:38; Heb 10:12-18). The bad news about human sin cannot be separated from the good news about God's forgiveness, and New Testament made clear that there is only one way this was made possible. This brings us to the third element of the "word of exhortation," a proclamation of God's message of salvation through Jesus's death and resurrection (Acts 13:26-31; Heb 9:11-28). Finally, a word of exhortation includes a warning against unbelief (Acts 13:40-41; Heb 2:1-4). These are just few of the things the pastor as exegete/prophet can preach.

In the Old Testament, the messages of the prophets include hope and judgment. The prophet Isaiah, who declared judgment against those who are not willing to distinguish right from wrong (Isa 5:20), is the same prophet who preached, "Comfort my people" (40:1). The prophet Jeremiah, who called out those who practice injustice (Jer 22:13), is the same prophet who assured the Jews of God's presence even with the certainty of exile (30:11). The prophet Ezekiel, who exposed the people's sins of murder and adultery (Ezek 22:3), is the same prophet who told the exiles about their return to Jerusalem (37:11–14). The prophet Daniel, who confessed that the people had broken the Law of Moses and therefore deserved God's punishment (Dan 9:4–19), is the same prophet who announced that the period of exile would soon be over (9:2). We can continue on with this list of examples, but these are enough to show that the sermons of the prophets were not always about "fire and brimstone," nor were they always about God's love and hope. Their message is a balance of both.

John R. W. Stott admits that preachers always have to struggle between "truth with unpopularity and falsehood with popularity."[3] He notes that the gospel still offends, and preachers cannot avoid disturbing people with its message. Yet he acknowledges the importance of meekness and gentleness in preaching.

> Every Christian pastor today should have the same feelings of tender love toward those who have been committed to his care. As we speak to them every Sunday, we know of some of the burdens they are bearing. As we look at their faces, we know that almost everybody has been bruised by life. We know they are feeling the pressure of temptation, defeat, depression, loneliness or despair. While it is true that some need to be disturbed from their self-satisfaction, others need the comfort of God's love above all else.[4]

Pastors as exegete/prophet must aim for this delicate balance between God's judgment of sin and a hope of forgiveness, and admonition to shun evil and exhortation to do good. These are the things that the pastor as a prophet must aim to have in his preaching, keeping in mind that messages of judgment must include a call to restoration and that messages of hope must include a call to repentance.

---

3. Stott, *The Challenge of Preaching*, 90.
4. Stott, *The Challenge of Preaching*, 92.

Accuracy

The Scripture is our only authoritative basis for preaching. This is not to suggest that we have nothing to learn from other disciplines or from other religions. Practicing humility means Christians must admit that there is a lot to learn from other sources. However, when it comes to Christian practices and beliefs, the Bible is our only source. The pastor as exegete/prophet has the responsibility to preach from the Scripture and to aim for accuracy.

Competence in Scripture and eloquence are two important qualities a preacher must aim to develop. The preacher should not really have to choose between eloquence and content; but having eloquence and some knowledge of Scripture without accurate understanding of God's truth is dangerous. Luke tells us about Apollos, an Alexandrian Jew who was knowledgeable in Scripture and a good orator (Acts 18:24); a combination of these two qualities should make a good preacher. Despite having these qualities and a boldness to preach the Scripture in the synagogue, Priscilla and Aquila saw him, "took him aside and explained to him the way of God *more accurately*" (18:26, italics added). Luke's statement suggests that despite Apollos's competence and eloquence, he initially lacked accuracy and that the couple saw the need to instruct him.

With advancing technology, a lot of members can easily check the accuracy of the information we present using their smart phones, whether it be the illustrations we use or the historical data related to the passage we present. This adds to the challenge of preaching in this era. However, more important than the accuracy of information we present is the truthfulness of the teachings we pass on. We should not only aim to present *facts*; we should present *truths*. Every preacher has and will at certain points in their preaching ministry say something incorrect, whether it be doctrine or information. If the mistake was doctrinal, since the error was made from the pulpit, the right thing to do is to correct it from the pulpit as soon as we are made aware of the error. This is one of the reasons why there is a need for theological education for preachers. However, there is more to accuracy than the *information* we present, we have to consider our *intention* as well. Haddon W. Robinson describes accuracy this way, "Accuracy, as well as integrity, demands that we develop every possible skill to keep us from declaring in the name of God what the Holy Spirit never intended to convey."[5] Inaccuracy has to do more with presumptuousness rather than imprecise information. When the pastor's personal agenda is given more weight than what the passage really teaches, there is a serious problem.

---

5. Robinson, *Biblical Preaching*, 62.

Diligence in studying the Scripture is one way to make sure we present Scripture's truth accurately. Paul reminded Timothy to make sure to handle the word of God carefully (2 Tim 2:15). "Accuracy" in preaching requires diligence in the study of the Word. Diligence in examining the Scripture is also one of the two things that made the Bereans more noble than the Thessalonians. Luke describes the Berean Jews, "Now these Jews were more noble than those in Thessalonica; they received the word with all eagerness, examining the Scriptures daily to see if these things were so" (Acts 17:11). The other reason is their willingness to listen even to those who may have different views and their unwillingness to allow their zeal for the truth cause them to harm others. Paul's message about the resurrection was not palatable for his Jewish contemporaries; even in the case of Peter, the point of contention between him and the religious leaders in Jerusalem was his message about the resurrection of Jesus (4:1–2). For the priests and Sadducees, the message about the resurrection is heretical! The Jewish Thessalonians also did not find the message of Christ's resurrection acceptable, but the Bereans carefully searched the Scripture whether Paul's message of the resurrection is true. The Thessalonian Jews, out of their zeal, caused a riot against Paul after hearing Paul preached about the resurrection (17:2–5); not content with that, they followed Paul to Berea and caused another riot (17:13). These are what makes the Bereans more noble than the Thessalonians.

Accuracy must be coupled with humility and respect for others who may have different views. This was the attitude of the Bereans as they listen to teachings that the faithful Jews considered heretical; all the more, this should be our attitude when discussing issues wherein the Scripture is not thoroughly clear. Aiming for accuracy should not blind us to the fact that there are various Christian traditions that developed in different regions throughout the centuries, and that the same Scripture was received in various ways. Conversely, the Scripture has set a clear boundary between truth and error which cannot be negotiated. All these is to say that in order for pastors to *be accurate* in preaching, they must *be diligent* in studying the Scripture and listening to others, and they must *be humble and respectful* even to those who view some issues differently.

Kneel

As we have seen earlier, although the ability to communicate clearly is important, preaching is not about one's eloquence. It is about faithfully delivering God's message through his empowerment. For this reason, total dependence on God is vital. The Scripture provides numerous examples of people who prayed or asked for prayers as they preach God's Word.

Paul requested the Colossians to pray for *opportunities to preach* (Col 4:3). He also asked the Thessalonians to pray so that the *gospel may spread quickly* (2 Thess 3:1). The filling of the Holy Spirit gave believers in Jerusalem *boldness in preaching*, and this happened after they prayed (Acts 4:31).

Contemporary style of worship is often criticized for being more like a concert than a worship service. There is truth to this criticism, although in many cases, the criticism is more stereotypical and exaggerated, rather than thoughtful and loving. We often ignore the fact that while some congregations find entertainment through praise and worship, others find entertainment through the performance of the preacher. Some are entertained by the music; some are entertained by the message. The fact that John of Antioch was nicknamed Chrysostom attests to the fact that congregations naturally crave for preachers with great oratorical skills. Even today, many churches that *prefer* traditional style of worship also *prefer* persuasive speakers. An image of a truth-loving and Scripture-centered congregation can guise the craving for oratorical entertainment and the tendency to be personality-centered that focused on the eloquent pastor. Oratorical skills of the speakers can captivate the audience, and their charismatic personality can cause the congregation to believe everything that they say, give whatever they ask, and do whatever they require. The pulpit ministry, however, is not about the preacher's stage presence but the presence of God; it not about their style but about substance of their message; and it is not about the personality of speaker but about power of the Spirit. The author of Hebrews describes God's word this way, "For the word of God is living and active, sharper than any two-edged sword, piercing to the division of soul and of spirit, of joints and of marrow, and discerning the thoughts and intentions of the heart" (Heb 4:12). Since the word of God is the sword of the Spirit (Eph 6:17), only the Spirit can wield it effectively. Bryan Chapell comments, "The work of the Spirit is as inextricably linked to preaching as heat is to the light a bulb emits. When we present the light of God's Word, his Spirit performs his purpose of warming, melting, and conforming hearts to his will."[6] After elaborating on the work of the Spirit, Chapell continues,

> These truths challenge all preachers to approach their task with a deep sense of dependence on the Spirit of God. Public ministry true to God's purposes requires devoted private prayer. We should not expect our words to acquaint others with the power of the Spirit if we have not met with him. Faithful preachers

---

6. Chapell, *Christ-Centered Preaching*, 33.

plead for God to work as well as for their own accuracy, integrity, and skill in proclaiming his Word. Success in the pulpit can be the force that leads a preacher from prayerful dependence on the Spirit. Congregational accolades for pulpit excellence may tempt one to put too much confidence in personal gifts, acquired skills, or a particular method of preaching. Succumbing to such a temptation is evidenced not so much by a change in belief as by a change in practice. Neglect of prayer signals serious deficiencies in a ministry even if other signs of success have not diminished. We must always remember that popular acclaim is not necessarily the same as spiritual effectiveness.[7]

In the Scripture, there were instances when the God's messenger proclaimed his message before those in authority. When Nebuchadnezzar had a troubling dream and he called for the sages in his court to interpret it, and because no one could explain its meaning to the king, he ordered that all the wise men be killed including Daniel and his three friends (Dan 2:1–15). Daniel requested for a meeting with the king to bring God's message to him, but he did so only after asking his three friends to pray *for his protection as he delivers God's message* (2:18). Jesus's promise to his disciples that the Holy Spirit would speak through them presumes that his disciples were also asking for God's mercy as they proclaim God's message before the rulers (Matt 10:17–20; Mark 13:11).

It is not only the messengers who need prayer, even the listeners need it. Paul did not only ask for God's favor as he preached, he also prayed for the believers so that they will understand God's message (Col 1:9), be able to apply it (1:10), and be able to find strength in God daily (1:11). Jeremiah prayed a similar prayer for his contemporaries (Jer 42:1–6).

THE PASTOR AS AN EXEGETE/PROPHET

The prophets in the Scripture are often viewed like a one-dimensional character in a story and the only thing they did was predict the future. This was the extraordinary task given to them, but it was clearly not the only thing they did. Prophets were preachers who brought God's message to his people, and the message they preached are not always new revelations from God but exhortations from the Law of Moses. In this sense, ancient prophets were exegetes who interpreted the Scripture available to them; they were preachers who proclaimed God's message to his people.

---

7. Chapell, *Christ-Centered Preaching*, 33.

There are similarities between the tasks of the prophets and that of the pastors. They are both preachers and interpreters of God's word. The pastors as exegete/prophet must SPEAK:

- Scripture: They must preach with a conviction that the Bible is the only authoritative source of teaching for the Christian life and doctrine.
- Persevere: Knowing that the people's response varies, pastors must persevere regardless of the people's response.
- Exhort: Preachers must distinguish between preaching the truth with boldness even if it offends and preaching to offend. The gospel is inevitably offensive, but sermons are basically "word of exhortation."
- Accuracy: A significant portion of preaching is the content; thus, the preacher must present the message accurately.
- Kneel: No amount of eloquence can transform the hearts of the people. Only God's Spirit has the power to do so.

Questions for Personal Reflection

Scripture: What does it mean to consider the Scripture as the sole authority for the Christian life and doctrine? Are there things we can learn from other religious groups? What does it mean to recognize that truths can be found in sources other than the Bible and having the Bible as the basis for preaching?

Persevere: What kind of negative responses have you or preachers you know received from members of the congregation? How can we distinguish people who refused to believe the gospel message, from critics who simply want to find fault, from those who critique constructively, and from people who choose only what they want to accept? Should we respond differently to these groups?

Exhort: How can we determine whether people are offended with our message because the truths we are presenting are unpalatable or because of our tactlessness, rudeness, and condescending attitude?

Accuracy: Is there a distinction between basic facts and biblical truths? What does it mean to be accurate in preaching?

Kneel: Recall the circumstances when you are tempted to not depend on the Spirit's empowering as you share God's word. How can you avoid the temptation to not depend on God when similar circumstances arise?

7

The Pastor as an Evangelist/Apologist

All mission work and evangelism spring from this intent, the redemptive purpose of the Savior-Shepherd to fill His sheep pen with all for whom He died. Pastors and missionaries together serve that purpose. They proclaim the one gospel under the same commission (Matt. 28:19). In Christ their work is one.[1]

—ROGER S. GREENWAY

JESUS BEGAN HIS MINISTRY by preaching in Galilee (Matt 4:17), and within the few years of his earthly ministry, he only preached within the regions of Galilee and Judea (4:23; 19:1). His goal, however, is for the gospel to be preached "to all nations" (28:19). It is impossible for one person to reach this goal. No wonder Jesus trained several men to continue his work even after he is gone. Jesus had many disciples during his time on earth, but he selected twelve men to train to do the work he was doing and to continue whatever he left unfinished.

The task is not just for the first group of Jesus's disciples. The New Testament shows us that the succeeding generations of disciples understood that this work must continue. Peter preached to the Jews in Jerusalem and the Diaspora (Acts 2:5–11), and to the Samaritans (8:25); Philip to the

---

1. Greenway, "Jesus, the Pastor-Evangelist," 97.

Samaritans and to an Ethiopian eunuch (8:5; 8:26–39); and Paul to the Jews scattered abroad and to the Gentiles (Acts 13–28). The apostles did not just exemplify the proclamation of the Gospel, like Jesus, they commanded and trained the next generation of believers to do the same (e.g., 2 Tim 4:2).

It is incorrect to assume that evangelism is a work only for pastors or missionaries; every believer must be involved in proclaiming the Gospel. It is also incorrect to assume that pastors minister only *inside* the church and the believers are the ones who should be doing the work of evangelism *outside*. Evangelism is an essential part of the pastoral ministry. No wonder Paul commanded Timothy to preach the Gospel in season and out of season (4:2). In evangelism, the pastor CALLS people to respond to Jesus's invitation: they Convince people to believe in Christ, Announce the good news that God is king, Labor to proclaim the Gospel, Lead them to the hope of eternal life by pointing them to the Savior, and Struggle to defend the faith by being ready to give an answer those who have questions about the Christian faith.

AN EVANGELIST/APOLOGIST CALLS

Convince

In the previous chapter, we discussed the importance of prayer in relation to preaching because preaching is not primarily about being eloquent nor is it merely about developing a good style of presenting a message. Preaching is essentially the Spirit's work in the mind and heart of the listeners. The same can be said about evangelism. Paul admits that human wisdom is not enough to convince people about the importance of Jesus's death and resurrection (1 Cor 1:17). Thus, the evangelist must trust in the Spirit's work more than his ability to persuade people.

However, the fact that the result of evangelism is dependent on the work of the Holy Spirit should not keep us from seeing that evangelism also involves persuasion. Paul claims, "Therefore, knowing the fear of the Lord, we *persuade* others" (2 Cor 5:11, italics added). Luke describes Paul's evangelistic work as an attempt to persuade both Jews and Greeks about the kingdom of God and to believe that Jesus is the Messiah (Acts 18:4, 13; 19:8, 26). Interestingly, the Greek language shows the close relation between persuasion, believing, and obedience. The verb *peithō* means "to persuade." Several passages show this:

1. Paul in Corinth: "And he reasoned in the synagogue every Sabbath, and tried to *persuade* Jews and Greeks." (18:4)
2. Paul in Ephesus: "And he entered the synagogue and for three months spoke boldly, reasoning and *persuading* them about the kingdom of God." (19:8)
3. Paul in Rome: "When they had appointed a day for him, they came to him at his lodging in greater numbers. From morning till evening he expounded to them, testifying to the kingdom of God and *trying to convince* them about Jesus both from the Law of Moses and from the Prophets." (28:23)

One who is persuaded is one who believes or trusts. There are several instances when *peithō* is translated "believe" or "trust." The religious leaders mocked Jesus for being convinced of God's deliverance (Matt 27:43a). In another instance, when Jesus asked the religious leaders about the source of John the Baptist's authority, they could not give him a straight answer because they were afraid of the people who believed (were convinced) that John was a prophet (Luke 20:5-6). Many Thessalonians believed (were persuaded) the message of Paul and Silas (Acts 17:4).

Persuasion also leads to obedience (e.g., Acts 5:36-37; Rom 2:8; Heb 13:17). Disobedience and unbelief are expressed in terms of being "unpersuaded" (*apeitheō*). Even the noun *apeitheia* can be translated "unbelief" (e.g., Rom 11:30, 32; Heb 4:6, 11) and "disobedience" (e.g., Eph 2:2; 5:6; Col 3:6). Although there is a word for the adjectives "unbelieving" or "unbelief" (*apistos*) and for the verb "disbelieve" (*apisteō*), sometimes the contrast in the New Testament is not between those who believe (*pisteuō*) and those who do not believe (*apisteō*), but between those who believe (*pisteuō*) and those who are unpersuaded/disobedient (*apeitheō*), "Whoever believes (*pisteuō*) in the Son has eternal life; whoever does not obey (*apeitheō*) the Son shall not see life, but the wrath of God remains on him" (John 3:36).

Luke describes Paul's evangelistic work as an attempt to persuade. While in Corinth, Paul "reasoned in the synagogue every Sabbath, and tried to persuade Jews and Greeks" (Acts 18:4). Likewise, in Ephesus where Paul spent three months, he would go to the synagogue "reasoning and persuading them about the kingdom of God" (19:8). Even Agrippa II, after several conversations with Paul about the kingdom of God, observed what Paul was trying to do, "In a short time would you persuade me to be a Christian?" (26:28).

Persuasion is an essential part of evangelism. The goal of which is to convince people, through the Spirit's work, in order that they may believe and be obedient because those who are unpersuaded will not believe and will not obey. The role of the evangelists, therefore, is to announce the

Gospel with the purpose of convincing their hearers about the person and work Jesus with the goal of seeing them believe and obey him. Evangelism is persuading people to change their beliefs, their commitments, and their lifestyle.

Announce

Not much was said about the ministry of John the Baptist, but the writers of the Gospel agree that the central point of John's message is about the kingdom of God (Matt 3:2; Mark 1:15). After John preached, "Repent, for the kingdom of heaven is at hand" (Matt 3:2), Jesus also did the same thing: "From that time Jesus began to preach, saying, 'Repent, for the kingdom of heaven is at hand'" (4:17). Before Jesus sent out his disciples, he instructed them to do the same: "And proclaim as you go, saying, 'The kingdom of heaven is at hand'" (10:7). For forty days after the resurrection, Jesus continued to preach about the kingdom of God to his disciples (Acts 1:3). Philip preached "the good news of the kingdom of God" to the Samaritans (8:12). Paul traveled bringing the same message (19:8; 20:25); and even when he was under house arrest in Rome, Luke recalls, "From morning till evening he expounded to them, testifying to the kingdom of God and trying to convince them about Jesus both from the Law of Moses and from the Prophets" (28:23), and for two years, Paul was "proclaiming the kingdom of God and teaching about the Lord Jesus Christ with all boldness and without hindrance" (28:31).

The good news that these evangelists announced is *God is king*! This is one of the important elements in evangelism. On several occasions, Jesus also claimed that he shares God's authority. In the story of Jesus's temptation, Satan offered to give Jesus all the kingdoms of the world in exchange for his worship (Matt 4:8–10). Satan had no authority to give what he promised to Jesus. Twice Jesus claimed that it is the Father, whom he called "Lord of heaven and earth," who gave him all authority in heaven and on earth (11:25–27; 28:16). The same Jesus invited everyone to be under his yoke (11:29–30). He was clearly speaking metaphorically. In the Old Testament, the metaphor of the yoke means to be under one's rule (Num 25:5), and often refers to oppressive regimes (Isa 9:4; 14:25; Jer 27:8, 11–12; 28:2, 4). It can also be burdensome (1 Kgs 12:4, 9–11, 14; 2 Chr 10:4, 9–11, 14). Jesus offered himself as king and invited everyone to be under his rule. Unlike the oppressive rulers, his yoke is easy and his burden is light. This is the message of hope we announce, and it is clear where this hope can be found. The evangelist's task is to point others to the source of hope. This brings us to the next element of evangelism—leading others to this source.

Lead

The evangelist's task includes leading the people to the source of hope. Jesus's calling of his first disciples is a brief story that illustrates the task of evangelism. When John the Baptist saw Jesus, he directed the attention of two of his disciples to Jesus, introducing him as "the Lamb of God!" (John 1:36). One of these two disciples was Andrew, who not only began to follow Jesus, but also pointed others to him (1:41–42a). What John and Andrew did exemplifies what every believer must do—lead others to the Messiah. The pastor as an evangelist must do the same.

Evangelism is, essentially, pointing others to the Messiah. We believe in Jesus because someone pointed us to him, whether it be a family member or a friend or even a stranger. Aside from John the Baptist and Andrew, many of those who found the Messiah (or were found by him) pointed others to him. The Samaritan woman, for example, after her conversation with Jesus went back to her town to announce what she found (4:28–29). After her encounter with the Christ, she was emboldened to tell others what she found. Her courage can be contrasted with her earlier tendency to avoid people. She drew water on the "sixth hour" (4:6), the time of day when it is normally the hottest, presumably the time of day when no one else was drawing water. The shame brought by her questionable relationships might have kept her from wanting to meet people, until she met Jesus. One may wonder how many Samaritans share her struggles or were looking for a hope when the woman spread the news about the Messiah. Rick Richardson observes,

> In the church we often think that our greatest strengths are our victories and successes. We don't even want to expose our faith to another unless we have things all together. In evangelism classes we spend much time training people to know the right answers but very little time teaching people to ask the right questions, of God, others and themselves. We've got it backwards. People will let us in if they feel we have shared their struggles. People will identify with our humanity if we will share it.[2]

Evangelism is essentially pointing others to the source of hope. The Samaritan woman did this. The man with leprosy did the same. After he was

2. Richardson, *Reimagining Evangelism*, 69.

healed, despite Jesus's command not to tell anyone about what happened except to the priest who would perform the cleansing rites, the healed man "went out and began to talk freely about it, and to spread the news" (Mark 1:45a). On another occasion, after Jesus healed two blind men, "they went away and spread his fame through all that district" (Matt 9:31).

One of the challenges pastors have to face is that the longer they are in ministry, and the longer they serve among the church goers, the less contact they will have with those who needed to hear the Gospel. This means that unless the pastors take a conscious effort to go out and do evangelistic work, their opportunity to share the Gospel will be limited. Richardson has some recommendations.

> If you are a pastor or another kind of Christian leader, the best thing you could do is skip some church stuff (or cancel some church stuff!) to do fun stuff and be with people far from God. Maybe nothing else would refresh and refuel you like doing what you love and being with people who aren't churchy. If you would do it, your people would do it. I know it's threatening to think about encouraging people to skip some church activities. But we Christians are ingrown and parochial and overwhelmingly stressed out by our busyness—working, attending church, being with church friends and family, and taking ourselves way too seriously all along the way.[3]

It is about intentionality. In the Gospels, we can see Jesus exerting an effort to go to the people who needed to hear the good news. He intentionally passed through Samaria where he met the woman with five husbands (John 4:4). After he preached in Nazareth, Jesus told his disciples, "I must preach the good news of the kingdom of God to the other towns as well; for I was sent for this purpose" (Luke 4:43). After which he went from Galilee to Judea to continue his work of proclaiming the good news.

Labor

Both Jesus and Paul talk about evangelism in terms of "labor" in a sense that it requires diligence and effort. Jesus asked his disciples to pray for the Lord of the harvest to send *laborers* (Matt 9:37–38). Likewise, Paul also viewed his ministry as *labor*. Talking about his missionary activities, Paul said, "If I am to live in the flesh, that means fruitful labor for me. Yet which I shall choose I cannot tell" (Phil 1:22). He also encouraged the believers to

---

3. Richardson, *Reimagining Evangelism*, 72.

continue growing in their faith so that his labors would not be in vain (2:16; see also 1 Cor 15:58; 2 Cor 11:23; 1 Thess 3:5). Paul's effort is seen, not only in his willingness to travel long distances and face extreme danger, but also in his willingness to make necessary adjustments in the way he presented the Gospel to different groups.

Paul's central message did not change, only the manner by which he presented his message changed. Take his presentation of the Gospel message to a Jewish audience (Acts 13:16–41) and to a gentile audience (17:22–32) as an example. When he shared the Gospel to the Jews, he addressed them as "those who fear God" (13:16); while he acknowledged the Gentiles as religious people (17:22). In referring to God among the Jews, Paul acknowledged that the God he worshipped is the God of their forefathers (13:17), implying a special relationship; while to the Gentiles, he referred to God using a more inclusive language, "the Lord of heaven and earth" who created everything, including the Gentiles (13:22). He referred to Israel as the nation chosen by God out of the many nations (13:18–19); then acknowledged that the Gentiles/nations that came from one man (17:26). In citing authoritative sources, he quotes from the Scripture among the Jews (13:22); but referred to a poet among the Greeks (17:28), not because Paul did not have a high view of the Scripture but because he was trying to communicate in a way that the Gentiles can understand. Nonetheless, to both Jews and Gentiles, his central message is about repentance (13:23–24; 17:29–31) and the resurrection (13:30; 17:32).

Paul is not the only one who was willing to present the same Gospel flexibly. Jesus talked about eternal life to Nicodemus, the Samaritan woman, and the rich young ruler. Jesus told Nicodemus that he must be born again (John 3:3). As a Jew, Nicodemus knew that he was also a recipient of God's promise to Abraham. Although Jesus did not discount God's special grace for the Jewish people, his statement implies that it is not enough for Nicodemus to be *born a Jew*, he must be *born again* to receive God's promise of eternal life. To the Samaritan woman, however, Jesus did not require her to be born again. Instead, he asked her to drink the living water to receive the same eternal life he promised to Nicodemus. Clearly, Jesus was not preaching a "different Gospel," he was simply presenting the same message in a different way. The Samaritan woman cannot make the same claim like Nicodemus, and her life even showed her spiritual thirst. No wonder Jesus asked her, not to be born again, but to drink the living water (4:13–14). The rich young ruler also asked Jesus about eternal life, and for this young man, his wealth kept him from becoming a follower of Jesus. Jesus did not ask him to be born again, nor to drink of the living water. Instead, he was told to sell his possessions to receive eternal life (Matt 19:21). Is this a Gospel of works? Not at all! In all three instances, the central message is the same: Jesus is the only object of faith (John 3:15, 16, 18), the only source of life (John 4:10, 13–14), and the only one to follow (Matt 19:21). There is no such thing as a one-size-fits-all method of evangelism, but there is definitely only one Gospel message.

The need for flexibility is part of our labor. Let me illustrate this further. The materials of *Evangelism Explosion* have been useful in many parts of the world, including the Philippines. Although memorizing a long script could be challenging for many, but a ready-made method is indeed helpful. The method, however, cannot be used without any adjustments. Take for example, the old Chinese immigrants in the Philippines. The topic of death is considered offensive. Thus, when the evangelist opens the conversation with, "If you die today," the conversation will be over before the evangelist finished asking the first diagnostic question. Some Chinese pastors recommended changing the question to, "A hundred years from now, where do you think will you be?" Only a few people live that long. The elderly person will already understand that the evangelist is talking about death, but the thought of what can possibly happen after a hundred years is better than talking about dying the very day they hear the Gospel. This is asking about death without having to ask the elderly person, "If you die today." We should not confuse between compromising the message and being flexible with the method. Flexibility is part of our labor.

Struggle

Evangelism is hard work. No wonder Jesus and Paul used "labor" as image to describe it. Evangelism can be challenging. One of the reasons is because even until today, various forms of persecutions await those who preach the good news. Paul's final letter to Timothy includes a command to preach the word in season and out of season (2 Tim 4:2), and this instruction, "As for you, always be sober-minded, endure suffering, *do the work of an evangelist*, fulfill your ministry" (4:5, italics added). He said this after reminding Timothy that many people will prefer myths over sound teachings (4:3–4). This implies that as an evangelist, Timothy must be ready to reason out and explain why certain beliefs are consistent with the teachings of the Scripture and why others are not. As an evangelist, he must also be ready to be an apologist. The need for a pastor to be ready as an apologist is greater considering the pluralistic world in which we live. Frances Adeney describes today's situation this way:

The increasing diversity in our society demands Christians' attention. As our world changes, our call to share the good news of the gospel molds itself to our new situations. As religious pluralism increases and we find Muslims, Hindus, and Buddhists in our neighborhoods and our schools, we need to consider what our responses will be. How will we, as individuals and communities, interact with our neighbors of other religions? As diversities of lifestyle increase, how will we reach out to people who live in forms of family or community, different from our own? As mobility continues to increase, how will our churches relate to neighborhoods that change even if we stay in one place?[4]

Aside from religious pluralism, Adeney points out four other challenges Christians face as they do the work of evangelism: a relative notion of truth, fundamentalist/modernist controversy that divides the church, postcolonial critiques of Western Christian missions, and a mishandling of evangelism by charlatans.[5] Adeney may be writing about the situation in the United States, but these challenges are also true even in other parts of the world. Hence, there is a need for Christians to be ready to do the work of an evangelist/apologist.

Jude gave a similar command to all believers (Jude 3). He explains that there were certain people who were spreading wrong doctrines. Both Jude and Paul used the metaphor of fighting or struggling to make their point: Jude tells the believers to "contend for the faith" (Jude 3), and Paul commands Timothy to "Fight the good fight of the faith" (1 Tim 6:12). Defending the faith is the task of all believers, and pastors have the responsibility as a believer and as a trainer of other believers. Pastors as evangelists need to struggle against ideas and teachings contrary to those of the Scripture, and this is where their role as apologists come in.

As Jude warns against false teachers, he mentions some of their characteristics which include scoffing (v. 18), faultfinding, and arrogance (v. 16). The pastors as apologists must keep this in mind, lest in their attempt to defend the faith against the false teachers, they share the same attitude of these false teachers. Peter advises, "but in your hearts honor Christ the Lord as holy, *always being prepared to make a defense* to anyone who asks you for a reason for the hope that is in you; yet *do it with gentleness and respect*" (1 Pet 3:15, italics added). There are those are genuinely looking for answers to their questions like the Ethiopian eunuch (Acts 8:30–36), and there are those who simply like to play the role of the devil's advocate like

4. Adeney, *Graceful Evangelism*, 56.
5. Adeney, *Graceful Evangelism*, 57.

the Pharisees, Herodians, and Sadducees (Matt 22:15–16, 23, 34). In either case, the pastor as apologist must be ready to answer their questions with gentleness and respect.

THE PASTOR AS AN EVANGELIST/APOLOGIST

The task of evangelism is far from over. Churches must continue to participate in this task, and the pastors have the responsibility to lead the church in this effort. The challenges we face vary from place to place and era to era. As an evangelist/apologist, the pastors need to be aware of the challenges their church is facing as they do this work, and to trust God in finding ways to overcome these various difficulties.

Religious pluralism, relativism, and cult groups are few of the challenges we face as we carry out the task of evangelism. Thus, an evangelist must be ready to be an apologist. As an evangelist/apologist, the pastor CALLS the people to acknowledge the rule of God.

- Convince: Evangelism involves persuasion, and persuasion does not only affect one's thoughts, but it should affect the way the person lives.
- Announce: Evangelism is basically an announcement of the good news that God is king and that he reigns through his Messiah.
- Labor: Even as the evangelists/apologists face the challenge of rejection and persecution, they must continue to exert effort in doing the work.
- Lead: The goal of evangelism is to share the message of hope to every person, and point people to the Savior.
- Struggle: Contend for the faith. Defend it. Be ready to give an answer to those who ask about the hope we have. Do it with gentleness and respect.

Questions for Personal Reflection

Convince: What are some of the barriers we typically encounter as we persuade others to believe in Christ? How can we get past these hurdles?

Announce: What does it mean to announce Jesus as both Savior and Lord? Should we emphasize one more than the other?

Labor: What are some of the hindrances you face in doing the work of evangelism? How can we overcome these challenges and difficulties?

Lead: What are the typical problems people in your community encounter? How can we lead these people to the real source of hope for the problems they face?

Struggle: What are some of the questions normally raised by people to whom you share the gospel? How can we answer these questions?

8

The Pastor as a Theologian/Ethicist

[T]his division of labor between the intellectuals and theologians, on the one hand, and the pastors as practitioners and translators, on the other, departs from historical precedent. In the not-so-distant past, and in many of the church's richest traditions, the pastorate was considered one of the most scholarly of vocations.[1]

—GERALD HIESTAND AND TODD WILSON

BEGINNING FROM THE EARLY church fathers until the period of the Reformation, there seems to be no clear distinction between a theologian and a pastor. A theologian is also someone involved in ministry, and a minister is also engaged in theology. This is not to suggest that there is no difference between the two tasks, but it seems that the separation between a theologian's role and that of a minister is a modern development rather than a practice among clergies throughout the centuries.

Each generation of believers has their own set of questions that need answers from the Scripture. Hence, the ability to do theological reflections is essential for pastors. Systematic theology and biblical theology provide the foundation to do contextual theological reflection; the minister's task is to

---

1. Hiestand and Wilson, *The Pastor Theologian*, 12.

listen to the Scripture's voice and echo the same today. The task of the pastor as theologian is to promote PEACE: Proclaim the peace of God, Examine theological issues, Address social concerns, Contemplate on the extent of God's redemption, and Engage in theological conversations.

THEOLOGIANS/ETHICISTS PROMOTE PEACE

Proclaim

Paul encouraged the Philippians not to worry about anything, but to pray when there is something that makes their hearts unsettled, holding on to God's promise, "the peace of God, which surpasses all understanding, will guard your hearts and your minds in Christ Jesus" (Phil 4:9). The "peace of God" which Paul mentions here clearly refer to something people experience within the heart and mind. Peace can be a psychological/emotional experience. Isaiah talks about those who have peace of mind because it is focused on God, "You keep him in perfect peace whose mind is stayed on you, because he trusts in you" (Isa 26:3). Likewise, Jesus assures his disciples of his peace so that their hearts will not be troubled (John 14:27).

The "peace of God," however, goes beyond one's internal experience. In the Scripture, peace also has to do with the physical, social, and political aspects of one's life. Modern people do not usually talk about "physical peace," but Jesus spoke of healing to the bleeding woman as a form of peace, "Daughter, your faith has made you well; go in peace, and be healed of your disease" (Mark 5:34). This incident shows that God's peace includes the physical well-being of a person. Peace also has social and political elements because where there is injustice, there is no peace. Peace in the society can only happen if justice is upheld. So Isaiah says, "The way of peace they do not know, and there is no justice in their paths; they have made their roads crooked; no one who treads on them knows peace" (Isa 59:8). In short, peace encompasses all areas of human life.

Separating the spiritual aspect of our life from others is not the Scripture's vision for humanity. Although peace need not be dependent on external circumstances, hence, it is possible to talk about the peace of God "which surpasses all understanding" (Phil 4:9), it is not an excuse to ignore the other aspects of life where God's peace is needed. The pastor as a theologian must be willing to reflect upon various issues facing humans and proclaim God's offer of peace.

Through the prophet Jeremiah, God spoke against the prophets who proclaim "'Peace, peace,' when there is no peace" (Jer 6:14; 8:11; see also

Ezek 13:10). The reason there is no peace is because the prophets were not willing to address the sins of the people and their leaders, which is injustice. Jeremiah explains, "For from the least to the greatest of them, everyone is greedy for unjust gain; and from prophet to priest, everyone deals falsely" (Jer 6:13). This is the reason there is no peace. The pastor as a prophet must be willing to speak against national and individual sins, as well as social and structural evil. In order to do so, he must also wear the hat of a theologian to critically reflect upon these issues and address them according to the teaching of the Scripture.

There is an unnecessary wedge often placed between theological reflections and preaching. A contrast is often made between "the ivory-tower theologians" and "the hands-on preacher." The former is criticized for being impractical and unreachable, detached from the realities of life; and the latter for being ill-informed and unreflective. There may be some truth to these criticisms, but much of them spring from human's age-old inclination towards conceit. The pastor, as a theologian, must keep in mind that theological reflections and preaching go hand-in-hand and the tasks should not be separated. Hiestand and Wilson clarifies the goal of the pastor as theologian.

> Insofar as the ecclesial theologian writes as a pastor, the ecclesial theologian is not afraid through his theology. Here again, we contrast the ecclesial theologian with a stereotype of the academic theologian. Academic theology does not generally get preachy. There are exceptions of course. But on the whole, the academy prioritizes disinterested neutrality and frowns upon the sort of dramatics one finds in a Luther or the explicitly pietistic concerns of a Wesley. But the ecclesial theologian does not remove the clerical vestment when he takes up the pen. The pulpit is always in view, even if indirectly. Certainly, each pastor is different, and thus each pastor's written "preaching voice" will be different. But nonetheless, the ecclesial theologian carries the preacher's burden into his scholarship, resulting in earnest admonitions toward repentance, faith in Christ, love of God and neighbor, and personal holiness. Orthopraxy and doxology—not mere clarity—is the goal of the ecclesial theologian. As such, the ecclesial theologian's scholarship should call for both.[2]

Theological reflections cannot be separated from proclamation, and the proclamation of the theologians cannot exclude the message of peace that God offers.

---

2. Hiestand and Wilson, *The Pastor Theologian*, 93.

Examine

The basis of our theological reflection is the Scripture, and its teachings will never change; but the challenges believers face and the questions they ask may change or evolve. Hence, the pastors must be ready to do theological reflections in response to these questions. Often when we talk about theology, we think in terms of philosophical propositions such as what we find in systematic theology. However, there is more to theology than profound philosophical statements. Theology should not only address the curiosity of the intellectuals in the congregation, but the spiritual concerns of the flock. Pastoral care and theological reflections are inseparable. As Hiestand and Wilson also suggest,

> And not only does the social location of the pastoral vocation offer unique insight into the issues being discussed by contemporary theologians, it also unearths hitherto under- and unaddressed questions. Questions regarding family, friendship, marriage, singleness, parenting, dating, personal finance, idolatry, addiction, and more, while given some attention by theologians and scholars, are not given attention in due proportion to their pastoral import in the life of God's people. The ultimate *telos* of Christian theology is the edification of the church—and not simply the church in its broad universal sense (however true this might be), but the church as composed of individuals: the old widower, the young business executive, the married mother of children. Theology exists as a means of supporting the hard work of faith in the lives of such as these. The pastoral social location foregrounds this vital aspect of theology, and the ecclesial theologian self-consciously—and vocationally—embraces it and allows it to the direct his work.[3]

There are a few instances in Paul's letters when he expressed his theological ideas in creeds and confessions, statements of faith, or philosophical propositions. For instance, concerning the purpose of Christ's coming Paul said, "The saying is trustworthy and deserving of full acceptance, that Christ Jesus came into the world to save sinners, of whom I am the foremost" (1 Tim 1:15), and of Christ's humiliation and exaltation, "though he was in the form of God, did not count equality with God a thing to be grasped, but emptied himself, by taking the form of a servant, being born in the likeness of men. And being found in human form, he humbled himself by becoming obedient to the point of death, even death on a cross. Therefore God has highly exalted

---

3. Hiestand and Wilson, *The Pastor Theologian*, 89–90.

him and bestowed on him the name that is above every name, so that at the name of Jesus every knee should bow, in heaven and on earth and under the earth, and every tongue confess that Jesus Christ is Lord, to the glory of God the Father" (Phil 2:6–11). He spoke about the value of endurance this way, "The saying is trustworthy, for: If we have died with him, we will also live with him; if we endure, we will also reign with him; if we deny him, he also will deny us; if we are faithless, he remains faithful— for he cannot deny himself" (2 Tim 2:11–13). However, Paul's theological ideas were not always expressed in creedal statements, rather as pastoral exhortations.

Paul's letters to the Corinthians and Thessalonians are examples of how a pastor can do theological reflections to address the questions of the congregation. In both instances, it seems that the two local churches asked Paul for his insights on certain issues. To the Corinthians he wrote a letter, not only as a pastoral response to the relational problems among its members as reported to him by Chloe's household (1 Cor 1:11), but also as a theologically practical response to the issues they raised in their letter to him, "Now concerning the matters about which you wrote" (7:1). Their questions include issues related to abstinence (7:1), marriage (7:25), food offered to idols (8:1), spiritual gifts (12:1), and even collection for the saints (16:1). In Paul's letter to the Thessalonians, he also addressed certain issues brought to his attention such as the questions concerning the last days (1 Thess 5:1) and the return of Christ (2 Thess 2:1).

Each generation faces its own set of challenges, some of these are old issues that are resurfacing, while others are totally new. The first Christian council in Jerusalem was formed because new questions were raised. The circumcision of the Gentiles is something that was never addressed during the earthly ministry of Jesus or even during the first decade after his resurrection; but it was an issue that required urgent response, as we are told, "The apostles and the elders were gathered together to consider this matter" (Acts 15:6). Like the apostles and elders, the pastors must also be willing to consider the new challenges the churches may face. At times, the nature of the question may even require consultations with other theologians *who hold different views* so that decisions can be made after various perspectives have been heard (15:13).

Address

The role of the pastors as theologian, as we can see by now, is inseparable from their role as prophet. The prophet who preaches against individual sins does not ignore national and social sins; and the prophet who speaks about social concerns cannot do so without doing theological reflections.

Many evangelicals are not comfortable with the idea that Christians should address social concerns. However, it requires exegetical cherry-picking to ignore the portions in the Scripture that show the prophets and even Jesus addressing social concerns. There are lots of passages to remove from the Scripture to silence the Bible about social issues. Isaiah called Israel to avoid oppressing the orphans and widows (Isa 1:17); and Ezekiel was not oblivious to the murder and injustices that were happening in Israel and Judah (Ezek 9:9). Hosea spoke against business owners who oppress the people with their dishonesty (Hos 12:7); and Malachi spoke God's word against those who refused to give the wages of their hired workers (Mal 3:5). Jeremiah indicted those who mistreat foreigners, orphans, and widows (Jer 22:3); and Zechariah also warned those who devise evil (Zech 7:9–10). Amos addressed the evil of treating the poor like commodities that can be purchased (Amos 8:4–6); and Joel showed the evil of prostitution (Joel 3:3). This list of passages is by no means comprehensive, but it is enough to make obvious the answer to the question, "Should Christians address social issues?"

Perhaps another question that should be asked in relation to this is "Did Jesus address social issues?" The answer is *Yes, he did!* Luke tells us the story of the widow who offered the little money that she had (Luke 21:1–4). This passage is often interpreted as an example of sacrificial offering. While it is true that we can learn a lot about sacrificial offerings from this story, considering the context of the passage, however, one should see that the passage is not mainly about offerings. It is a story that shows us how Jesus addressed the problem of oppression of widows.

In the verses just before this story, we see Jesus telling his disciples not to imitate the scribes who are more concerned with the honor they receive and "who devour widows' houses and for a pretense make long prayers" (20:47). Immediately after Jesus told his disciples that the scribes were devouring widow's houses, the poor widow came to give her offerings. Jesus's conversation with his disciples (20:45–47) and the story of the widow's offering (21:1–4) should be considered as part of one story. Jesus honored the widow by describing her offering, "she out of her poverty put in all she had to live on" (21:4). The widow clearly needed help, and God kept reminding his people never to ignore those who are in need (Exod 22:22). Instead of helping her, the scribes were more concerned about their honor; and the fact that some had excesses means that they had enough help the widow in need, but they did not. The honor that the religious leaders and the wealthy people received for giving from their excesses is, according to Jesus, clearly undeserved. Jesus addressed social issues. The pastor as a theologian cannot ignore the questions we face in our society.

Contemplate

The problems humans face are consequences of human sins. As it is often said, "The heart of the problem is the problem of the heart." Jesus himself taught, "For out of the heart come evil thoughts, murder, adultery, sexual immorality, theft, false witness, slander" (Matt 15:19). Human sinfulness is expressed in various forms of violation of God's commands. The pastor as a theologian must be prepared to answer these moral and ethical questions that members of congregation may raise.

The Scripture may not directly address all the challenges and issues we face today, but God's commandments provide us with principles to guide us in making moral and ethical decisions. The Ten Commandments, no matter how simple they may seem, actually set these foundational principles as we address various issues today. The first command, "You shall have no other gods before me" (Exod 20:3), is essential in dealing with questions concerning religious pluralism. The second commandment, "You shall not make for yourself a carved image" (20:4), addresses questions relating to idolatry (that is, making God less than what he really is or making any of his creation more than what they really are), and indirectly, to human dignity (making humans less than creatures created in God's image). The third command, "You shall not take the name of the LORD your God in vain" (20:7), is more than just a prohibition to swear, but it has something to say about religious extremism (terrorism "in the name of God") and doctrinal fundamentalism (verbal abuse in the guise of defending the truth "in the name of God"). The fourth command, "Remember the Sabbath day, to keep it holy" (20:8), may be related to questions of slavery (which prohibits humans the kind of rest designed by God), and even ecology (God required even the land to rest [23:10–12]). The fifth command, "Honor your father and your mother" (20:12), is more than obeying the parents, but it is about honoring (not shaming) them, and has some bearing about the topic on caring for the elderlies. The sixth command, "You shall not murder" (20:13), clearly addresses issues like abortion and extra-judicial killing, not just premeditated murder. The seventh command, "You shall not commit adultery" (20:14), is a command against extramarital affairs, but its foundational principle of sexual propriety can address various forms of illicit behaviors like rape, incest, homosexuality, bestiality, among others. The eighth command, "You shall not steal" (20:15), shows the importance of valuing the properties of others. The ninth command, "You shall not bear false witness against your neighbor" (20:16), is the bedrock of human justice system because disobedience to this command leads to injustice. The tenth command, "You shall not covet" (20:17), answers questions related to materialism and consumerism.

Doing theology requires more than just an academic qualification. It should spring out of a conviction that God is the almighty Creator, the loving Father, and the righteous Judge whose standards of holiness humans are not able to meet, but out of his grace he provided a way for our redemption which should affect all areas of our life. Kevin J. Vanhoozer explains, "Theology is neither a nine-to-five job nor a career . . . The image you should have in mind is not the professor with a tweed jacket, but rather the disciples who dropped everything to follow Jesus. Becoming a theologian means following God's Word where it leads with all one's mind, heart, soul, and strength."[4]

In Paul's letter to the Romans, he explained to them the gravity of human sin and the extent of its effect. Paul explained how we humans fail to honor the one God (Rom 1:21) resulting in us dishonoring our own bodies (1:23); and having a depraved mind we engage in all kinds of evil practices that contradict God's commandments (1:28–31). Paul the theologian also explained to them the consequences of sin (3:23; 6:23), and God's solution to the problem of human sins (5:12–17). As a theologian, Paul also contemplated on the extent of God's redemption when he discussed the relationship between human sins and the rest of creation, our anticipated future and its implications for us today (8:18–30). God's salvation does not only include the hope of eternal life after we die, but an opportunity to experience God's presence while we still live. As Jesus explained eternal life, "And this is eternal life, that they know you, the only true God, and Jesus Christ whom you have sent" (John 17:3).

These are also some of the questions the pastors must constantly ask. The pastor as a theologian must not only contemplate the extent of human sin, but also the extent of God's redemption. Vanhoozer describes the ministry of pastor/theologian as a ministry of understanding. He writes,

> To minister understanding is to help people make connections: between the parts of the Bible and the overarching story; between; between the Bible and the world in which they live; between who they are and who God calls them to be. Pastors are called not to practice academic theology but to minister theological understanding, helping people interpret Scriptures, their cultures, and their own lives in relation to God's great work redemption summed up *in Christ*.[5]

---

4. Vanhoozer, "Letter to an Aspiring Theologian," 27–28.
5. Vanhoozer and Strachan, *The Pastor as Public Theologian*, 112.

Engage

Theologians, no matter how contemplative or observant, normally see things better when in conversation with others. Hence, it is important to be engaged in dialogue with others, especially with those who see some issues from a different standpoint. Paul is a good example of this. Despite being the recipient of God's special revelation concerning the Gentiles, Paul was humble enough to consult other church leaders to make sure he had the right teachings. He recalled his trip to Jerusalem after his encounter with the risen Christ, "I went up because of a revelation and set before them (though privately before those who seemed influential) the gospel that I proclaim among the Gentiles, in order to make sure I was not running or had not run in vain." (Gal 2:2).

Paul was clear about his convictions. This is seen, for instance, in his refusal to have Titus circumcised (2:3). He explained that some "false brothers" were unwilling to accept Jesus's offer of freedom from the Law, insisting that Titus must be circumcised even though he was a Gentile (2:2–3). In the case of Timothy (who had a Jewish mother and a Greek father), Paul was the one who circumcised Timothy (Acts 16:3). There is no indication that the Jews in Lystra and Iconium demanded Timothy to be circumcised, and Luke's account seems to suggest that Paul did not want Timothy's being uncircumcised be a hindrance to their ministry among the Jews. However, there was clearly pressure from the Jews from Jerusalem to have Titus circumcised because "he was a Greek" (Gal 2:3), presumably, both his parents were Gentiles. Paul was battling against the idea that Gentiles must be circumcised before they can be a follower of Jesus, and he stood his ground firmly for the sake of the gentile Christians. He told the Galatians, "to [the false brothers] we did not yield in submission even for a moment, so that the truth of the gospel might be preserved for you" (2:5).

The circumcision of the Gentiles was the main issue discussed in Acts 15. Although Paul was clear about his convictions and his stance on the matter came as God's direct revelation to him, he made himself accountable to the leaders of the church in Jerusalem by presenting to them the message he proclaimed among the Gentiles, apparently to make sure that he was not preaching something erroneous. As he claimed, he feared that all his efforts in preaching will amount to nothing if he did not preach what is true (Gal 2:2).

The world is constantly changing, and we may encounter ethical issues and challenges we have never encountered before. The pastor as a theologian/ethicist must be ready to address these. This task is great for one person to handle, and that is why there must be a concerted effort and a conversation among pastors to address the various issues of the day. This conversation need not be limited within the sphere of faith. Addressing ethical issues often require a dialogue between faith and other sources of knowledge. William C. Placher explains,

> When Christians address ethical problems, we should draw on the best expertise available. When we think about the world, most of us, most of the time, use the categories of contemporary natural and social science. If we do not connect our faith to those categories, we will end up compartmentalizing Christianity off in a corner and treating it as not about the real world.[6]

The difficulty in this type of engagement is that even among Christians who make their case from the Bible, we can expect differences in opinions and interpretation of the same Scripture. Hence, it is important to have a posture of a listener, both to the voice of Scripture and to interpretation of others. These differences should not stop us from engaging in discussions on ethics and doing theological reflections. Jonathan Leeman explains,

> What Christians need is a more careful form of *pastoral reasoning*. We need it for the purposes of engaging in the public square . . . But make no mistake, such pastoral reasoning is crucial for confronting all the ethical and countless practical decisions that confront us in day-to-day life. Pastoral reasoning works from the Scripture and employs theological principles. Yet what makes it distinct from biblical or theological reasoning is that it seeks answer "real-life" questions and help people make "real-time" decisions. It is one thing to exegete a text or that theological principle to life.[7]

THE PASTOR AS A THEOLOGIAN/ETHICIST

As the world continues to change, we face new issues and challenges that require us to ask ethical questions and do theological reflections. The pastor will not have the answer to all the questions, but there is no excuse not to reflect on what the Scripture says, whether directly or indirectly, about these concerns.

The pastor's task as theologian/ethicist is closely related to their responsibility as an exegete/prophet. The pastors who do theological reflections promote PEACE.

---

6. Placher, "Doubting Theology," 25.
7. Leeman, "The Need for Pastoral Reasoning," 40.

- Proclaim: The peace that God offers permeates every area of our life, and this is the peace we must proclaim.
- Examine: The Scripture is the source for answering questions about ethics and morality, hence, the pastor must carefully examine it.
- Address: The Scripture addressed both spiritual and social concerns. The pastor must discuss one without neglecting the other.
- Contemplate: The effects of human sin extend to all areas of our life, but so is God's redemption. The pastor as theologian must take seriously the extent that God's salvation.
- Engage: The pastor as theologian cannot do the work alone; thus, the constant need to be in conversation with others, whether they share our views.

Questions for Personal Reflection

Proclaim: Knowing that the pastor's task includes both theological reflections and proclamation, how does that affect the way you look at preaching? How does that affect the way you choose texts and topics for preaching?

Examine: How can we make sure that in our study of the Scripture, we allow the Scripture to speak, rather than impose our own agenda? In what ways do we silence the Scripture on certain issues? How can we avoid silencing the Scripture?

Address: What are some of the issues facing your community at present? Are they unique to your community or is it something that Christians from other parts of the world also face? How can you address these issues?

Contemplate: Considering the extensiveness of God's redemption, what difference does it make to the way you do theological reflections? Are there barriers that keep you from seeing and acknowledging the extent of God's salvation?

Engage: What hindrances do you experience that keep you from getting into theological conversations with other pastors? Is there any way to deal with these hindrances?

9

The Pastor as a Manager

> There is no question but that many pastors find tension within themselves in reconciling their roles as shepherds and as overseers . . . Yet effective coordination of the activities of people demands organization. And organization requires administration.[1]
>
> —W. T. Purkiser

One of the qualifications of elders in Paul's list is: "He must manage his own household well, with all dignity keeping his children submissive, for if someone does not know how to manage his own household, how will he care for God's church?" (1 Tim 3:4–5). This requirement implies two things: one of the elder's role is to manage the church (household of God), and they are not neglecting their own family (household of the elder). We will discuss the first one in this chapter and the second in the next.

Every local church should be able to come up with a list of activities they do regularly, and perhaps in this list of activities are some essential, some redundant, some unnecessary, and some neglected; and some are important and necessary but not in the said list. As a manager, the pastor

---

1. Purkiser, *The New Testament Image of the Ministry*, 125.

makes sure to take care of essentials, consolidate the redundant ones, discontinue the unnecessary, initiate the ones ignored, and revive the ones neglected. In short, the pastors as manager is responsible to set things in ORDER: Oversee the various ministries, Recruit faithful and able people, Delegate task to them, Envision the direction of the church, and Respond to ministry concerns.

MANAGERS SET THINGS IN ORDER

Oversee

When Paul was about to leave Ephesus because his life was in danger, he met with the *elders* of the local church to give instructions, "Pay careful attention to yourselves and to all the flock, in which the Holy Spirit has made you *overseers*, to *care* [literally, "to shepherd"] for the church of God, which he obtained with his own blood" (Acts 20:28, emphasis added). In other words, for Paul, the *elders* perform the work of an *overseer* and part of that is to *shepherd* (pastor) God's flock. The pastor, therefore, is the elder who oversees.

The designation of *overseer* for pastors clearly suggests that one of their tasks is to oversee the church. To oversee involves caring, giving attention to something or someone.[2] This definition has to do with meeting the spiritual needs of the congregation. No wonder, when Peter instructed the elders, he commanded them to "shepherd the flock of God that is among you, exercising oversight" (1 Pet 5:2). Shepherding is part of exercising oversight; and exercising oversight includes shepherding.

Moreover, by definition, an overseer is "one who has the responsibility of safeguarding or seeing to it that something is done in the correct way."[3] This description has to do with the various ministries of the church. Joshua's leadership provides some principles worth following. When Joshua was appointed as the new leader of Israel, he knew exactly his assigned task—to lead Israel into the Promised Land. God reminded him of this task, "Be strong and courageous, for you shall cause this people to inherit the land that I swore to their fathers to give them" (Josh 1:5). Likewise, as a manager, the pastor must be clear where he is leading the church. This means the pastor must make sure that the church does not do activities only for the sake of doing activities. He must be clear about the goals and purposes for each activity, consolidating those that are redundant, creating new activities

---

2. BDAG, s.v. "*episkopeō*."
3. BDAG, s.v. "*episkopos*."

to meet a particular need, and discontinuing those that already served their purpose.

Joshua did not assume the title of "overseer," but his deeds show that he functioned as one. As Joshua prepared to lead the people, even though he was leading a military expedition, his preparation focused more on God's Word rather than military strategy (1:7–8). Joshua crossed the Jordan to take the land of Canaan. From a human viewpoint, it is both risky and strategic. On the one hand, it is risky because crossing the Jordan means they would be caught in the middle having enemies both from the north and from the south. On the other hand, it is strategic because securing the central region as stronghold would make it difficult for tribes from the north to join forces with those from the south. Joshua's decision, however, was not based on the pros and cons, but on God's instruction. Even while they were wandering in the desert, God was already hinting to them that their point of entry to Canaan is through the Jordan (Num 35:10). This was also the instruction he gave through Moses (Deut 9:1; see also 11:31; 27:2). In the same way, while strategic planning is important, the primary goal of the pastor as a manager is to make sure that the ministry plans are consistent with God's standard.

Moreover, just before Joshua led the people to the Land, he consecrated them (Josh 3:5). As a manager, the pastor must also make sure that the right people are assigned to the right ministry. The gifts and abilities of the people serving in various ministries are important, but the spiritual condition of the person is of greater importance. Assigning people *only* on the basis of their abilities without considering their character may create problems for the church. This brings us to the second task of the pastor as manager—recruiting the right people.

Recruit

Pastors cannot do everything by themselves; they needed people to help them do the ministry. The pastors must not only recruit, they must (1) recruit the right people, (2) provide specific instructions on how to carry out the work, and (3) have a clear vision and direction for the ministries of the church. We will elaborate more about the second and third items later. In this section, let us discuss briefly about recruiting the right people.

Paul's letter to Titus, pastor of a church in Crete, has a clear purpose, "This is why I left you in Crete, so that you might put what remained into order, and appoint elders in every town as I directed you" (Tit 1:5). Paul's statement suggests a few things. First, there seems to be more than one local congregation in Crete. The Gospel must have already spread to different towns and there were groups of believers in these places that needed a pastor. The believers in these towns needed to grow in their faith, and they needed protection from the increasing number of false teachers in Crete, "For there are many who are insubordinate, empty talkers and deceivers, especially those of the circumcision party. They must be silenced, since they are upsetting whole families by teaching for shameful gain what they ought not to teach" (1:10–11).

Second, Paul's desire was for Titus to set things in order for these churches. The verb *epidiorthoō* translated as "set things in order" can also be translated "to rectify,"[4] this implies that problems need to be corrected. What were the problems? One of them was the lack of an overseer. Hence, the need for pastors to be appointed. The lack of pastors in the Cretan churches did not only make these congregations vulnerable to the attacks of false teachers, there was also no one to challenge the cultural weaknesses that made the Cretans gain the reputation of being "liars, evil beasts, lazy gluttons" (1:12). Thus, Paul instructed Titus to rebuke them (1:13).

Third, which is also related to the second one, the lack of pastor in these churches kept these churches from having order. No wonder Paul directed Titus to make sure that the people he would choose and appoint as elders could manage the household of God. Moreover, seeing that the Cretans have a problem of insubordination (1:10), Paul instructed Titus to teach the value of submissiveness (2:5, 9; 3:1).

Paul instructed Titus to recruit people with a clear set of guidelines on how to choose the right people (1:6–9). A comparison between the list of qualifications for elders and that for deacons in Paul's letter to Timothy shows that skills and abilities are important. The teaching responsibility of the elders requires them to be "able to teach" (1 Tim 3:2). Although this is not required for deacons, they are also expected to "hold the mystery of the faith with a clear conscience" and be faithful to God's word (3:9). The main similarity between the requirements for elders and for deacons is character. What this means is that the skill requirement for different types of ministries may vary, but there are character requirements for everyone who wanted to serve God. One may argue that there must be a stricter requirement for those who will be assuming leadership responsibilities in the church, but this does not mean that character is not a consideration for those taking other forms of ministry. In fact, we may argue that the "right people" are those who do not only possess the skill to perform the task, but more importantly the character required from any minister.

---

4. BDAG, s.v. "*epidiorthoō.*"

Paul "set things in order" for the body of Christ by directing Titus to "set things in order" for the churches in Crete—and this was by appointing overseers who could "set things in order" for each local church. What Paul did on a larger scale, the local church pastors should also do for the local churches in Crete. Having assessed the situation of the churches in Crete and having identified their need, he instructed Titus to take the steps to fill the leadership void in these churches. As mentioned earlier, there are usually more people who wanted to serve voluntarily in churches than those who are actually serving; some are hesitant for lack of training, and so the pastor as a teacher must find ways to train the members of the congregation. Similarly, many of those who have volunteered to serve may feel unsure what to do, and it is the responsibility of the pastor as an overseer to provide directions for their coworkers as they serve. This brings us to the third responsibility of the pastor as manager—delegation.

Delegate

We have discussed the importance of delegation in the chapter on *The Pastor as a Teacher/Trainer* and stressed that the main purpose of delegation should not be to help the pastor avoid burnout (although this is important, too); but pastors delegate because it is an essential part of training people. The pastor must delegate from the perspective of a teacher/trainer who wants to see members of their congregation fulfill the tasks God called them to do. The pastor must also do so with the eyes of an overseer who wants to see members of their congregation get involved in God's work, making sure they are assigned to ministries where they fit. The overseer must make sure the church is going the right direction and things are done according to scriptural standards. This part of being an overseer cannot be given to others. As managers, they must also see to it that the right people are in the right places, that the various ministries in the church are being done properly, and that no work is neglected. One person cannot fulfill all these. Thus, the pastor must delegate some of these responsibilities to faithful and capable people.

Joshua the overseer led Israel with a clearly defined task (lead the people to the Promised Land); he prepared himself with God's Word, and consecrated God's people for God's work. Joshua the manager also assigned tasks to the *people*. Israel's entry to the Promised Land required military expedition, and their military expedition required fighters. In many instances, God granted victory to Israel despite a small army size (e.g., Gideon's battle against Midian [Judg 7:1–18]). In this battle, however, the participation of all the twelve tribes was expected, and Joshua made sure that all tribes were involved, including the tribes that have already settled on the east side of the Jordan.

Delegation does not only require appointing people to a certain task, it also requires allotment of resources. Before entering the Land to take possession of it, Joshua instructed his officers to go through the camp to tell the people, "Prepare your provisions, for within three days you are to pass over this Jordan to go in to take possession of the land that the LORD your God is giving you to possess" (Josh 1:11). Aside from people, *provisions* are also needed to accomplish God's task. Joshua knew this; thus, he instructed the Israelites to prepare provisions with a clear time frame of "three days." Every ministry requires some kind of provision. Today, we call it "budget." Budgeting is part of good stewardship. We make budgets so that we do not overspend nor underspend. We are not being good stewards if we spend on things that are unnecessary. Conversely, underspending may look good on paper because it gives the appearance that there is savings, but there will be times when some ministries suffer if we do not spend what is necessary. Underspending that results from premature termination or unnecessary abandonment of any ministries is as bad as overspending due to extravagance and poor forecasting of expenditures; both are undesirable. Overspending that is due to unexpected growth of a ministry is as desirable as underspending that results from an increasing number of generous members supporting God's work. Underspending is not always a better form of stewardship than overspending, because good stewardship is spending the resources *for what is necessary*. Good stewardship is not spending more than what is needed even if we have a huge buffer and not holding back spending when it is needed even if we have a drying coffer.

Aside from appointing people and allotting resources, careful planning and execution are also part of delegation. Joshua appointed two spies to survey the land. His action shows that trusting God and careful *planning* are not mutually exclusive. A leader can trust God while making careful plans, and having careful plans does not imply a lack of trust. Absolute trust does not mean we can be reckless and thoughtless. Leaders who trust God are those who trust God as they make plans and execute them. They trust God from beginning to end. Joshua's action recalls Moses's sending of the twelve spies so that they may gauge the strength of the people they were about to face, identify areas of stronghold, and estimate the productivity of the land (Num 13:17–20). It seems that Joshua sent the spies for the same reasons. Now that Israel was about to enter the land, they needed information so that they could carefully plan their actions. In the same way, there are information that pastors must know first as they start or continue a particular ministry. In some cases, demographic analysis is even necessary. In the ministry, it is better to trust God *with* the information we need to be able to plan carefully than to trust God *without* the information.

Joshua the manager also reminded the two-and-a-half tribes of their promise to participate in the conquest, assigned officers to instruct the people to prepare to enter the Land, and sent spies to get the needed information so they can make strategic plans. The process of delegation also involves people, provisions, and planning. The pastor as a manager must also be ready to do these.

Envision

Although many believers are willing to give their time and effort in service, some are hesitant to serve because they are not sure what to do and how to get involved. It is the pastor's responsibility, as manager/overseer, to help the congregation to understand why they need to do what they are doing. Some people get involved in the work if they are told *what* to do; but more people get involved if they know *what* to do and *why* they need to do it. Hence, the pastors as manager must have a clear vision, and they must be able to communicate this vision to the people so that they can be clear why and how they can participate in it. There are three important characteristics of visionary leadership: (1) visionary leaders know what God wants to do; (2) they foresee the process how it can be done; and (3) they are able to bring people in to join the work.

The story of Nehemiah is often used as an example for visionary leadership; and for good reasons. He showed the characteristics of a visionary leader. Nehemiah was a good manager who understood God's desire for his people, knew what needs to be done and how to go about doing it, and was able to invite the people to participate in the task.

First, he knew what God wanted for his people. Nehemiah was given the credit for the rebuilding of the wall in Jerusalem after it was destroyed by the Babylonians. He had the conviction that his desire to rebuild the wall is something God placed in his heart (Neh 2:12). Moreover, he knew what is inconsistent with God's plan (6:12).

Second, Nehemiah knew what must be done and how to go about doing it. This process requires getting the facts related to the work. Prior to the planning and the actual rebuilding of the wall, Nehemiah investigated the condition of the Jews in Jerusalem (1:2–3). The wall was broken; there is a need to rebuild it. At this point, Nehemiah had to grapple with the question of the connection between the physical condition of Jerusalem and the spiritual condition of its people. As soon as Nehemiah heard the news, knowing that the wall was torn as a consequence of the nation's sins, he began confessing their sins (1:5–7), recalling God's promises (1:8–9), and asking his favor (1:10–11). Nehemiah's action suggests that his desire to rebuild the wall remains within the boundary of God's promises to his nation. In other words, Nehemiah had an ambition to rebuild the structure, but it was clearly not out of selfish desire that he wanted to do it.

Third, Nehemiah got the Jews involved in doing the work. Nehemiah went around the city and inspected the wall thoroughly (2:12–14). With a clear sense of God's mandate and with the information of the actual condition of the city, he spoke to the leaders of the people, "You see the trouble we are in, how Jerusalem lies in ruins with its gates burned. Come, let us build the wall of Jerusalem, that we may no longer suffer derision" (2:17). He was clear about what God was doing and the Persian king's favorable response to him further confirmed God's direction for him (2:18). He needed the people to get involved. Nehemiah 3 lists the people who willingly participated in the work and were placed in charge of repairing particular sections of the wall with this assurance, "The God of heaven will make us prosper, and we his servants will arise and build" (2:20).

The desire to see God's task accomplished gave him the courage to talk with the Persian king (2:1–8), to make preliminary inspections and planning (2:9–17), to face oppositions (2:18–20), to mobilize people to do the work (3:1–32), to face more oppositions (4:1–14), to continue the work despite the challenges (4:15–23), to have the courage to face threats (6:1–14), and to finally complete the task (6:15–19). These cannot happen without a clear vision.

Respond

We have so far discussed four tasks of the pastor as a manager. These four tasks share a common element—predictability. The pastors as managers who oversee the ministries of the church must have a clear assessment of the needs of these ministries; they must have a clear list of expectations and qualifications of people to recruit; they must be intentional as they delegate tasks to their coworkers; and they must share to the congregation the vision of what they want to accomplish in their ministry. There is a certain degree of predictability in these tasks and their timing can be planned. However, sometimes needs arise unexpectedly. The pastor as a manager must be ready to respond to various needs, whether unforeseen or anticipated, urgent or delayable. Wisdom is needed to distinguish which needs require immediate response, which ones can be delegated and delayed, and the kind of responses needed. Needs that arise cannot simply be ignored, and the pastor as a manager must be up for the task.

There are a couple of things the pastor as a manager must remember in dealing with unexpected issues that may arise. First, *identify the root cause of the issue*. Luke candidly recounts the internal problem that the church in Jerusalem encountered as the size of the congregation grew. The conflict between the Greek speaking Jews and those speaking their native tongue in the church in Jerusalem put the apostles to test. The Hellenists complained that their widows were being neglected in the daily food distribution (Acts 6:1). The problem seems trivial because they were complaining about food; but the problem of food distribution is just the symptom of a more serious problem—the ethnic and cultural tension between Hebrew and Hellenist widows. The problem was not at all surprising because even in the Gospels, there are already indicators that racial tensions existed between the Jews and non-Jews (e.g., John 4:9). However, there is no indication that anyone in the church in Jerusalem expected this to happen. The apostles were ready to find resolution.

Second, *the pastors as manager must know their limitations and priorities*. The problem of racial tension cannot be solved overnight. It may never be resolved at all; but steps can be taken to at least minimize the tension. The apostles/elders in Jerusalem responded to this challenge, not by pretending that this racial/ethnic tension can be resolved immediately nor by ignoring that there was a problem. They tried resolving this by identifying their priorities and appointing deacons to make sure the needs of the Greek speaking widows were not neglected (Acts 6:2–4). A group of widows were being neglected. This issue that the Greek speaking Jews raised was not a trivial matter. They may not be directly involved in the distribution of food for the Greek speaking widows, but they "set things in order" by assigning able men to do it. Pastors as managers must also be ready to respond to the needs of the congregation, whether it be through direct involvement in the task or by appointing others to do so.

Third, *the pastors as managers must distinguish between short-term and long-term solutions, and identify the best solution for the situation*. As mentioned above, the ethnic and cultural tension between the Hebrews and Hellenists may never be fully resolved. Even until today, the conflict between different races and ethnicities is difficult to solve; and churches that claim to be multicultural tend to solve this problem by becoming multi-congregational. For the church in Jerusalem, assigning deacons to distribute food may not have solved the real issue, but the best solution for that situation was appointing representatives for the neglected widows. The lineup of deacons chosen to take the responsibility of food distribution is worth noting. The names of the deacons suggest that they had strong Hellenistic influence; one of them was even a proselyte, which means he was not a Jew (6:5). The appointment of the Hellenistic deacons shows that the apostles took seriously the complaints of the Hellenistic widows by assigning their representatives to make sure that they will not be neglected in the food distribution.

Responding to unexpected problems requires an attitude of a servant. In situations like this, the pastor may have to temporarily drop what they are doing to attend to these interruptions. It requires an attitude of a servant to be willing to do so.

THE PASTOR AS A MANAGER

The designation "overseer" for pastors presume they have to do the work of a manager. The list of qualifications for elders also imply that one of the pastor's responsibilities is administration, "He must manage his own household well, with all dignity keeping his children submissive, for if someone does not know how to manage his own household, how will he care for God's church?" (1 Tim 3:4–5).

The pastors who assume the role of a manager are responsible to set things in ORDER:

- Oversee: The pastor supervises the various ministries making sure every ministry is healthily growing and no ministry is neglected.
- Recruit: As a manager, the pastor must be attentive to find people who can serve in various ministries.
- Delegate: Pastors should not only identify people who can serve, they must also assign tasks suitable for them.
- Envision: It is not enough for pastors to know what to do and who will do them; it is important for them to know why the work must be done and to make this clear to the congregation.
- Respond: There will be times when the unforeseen happens. The pastor as a manager must be prepared to respond to these challenges.

Questions for Personal Reflection

Oversee: How can you assess if a ministry is healthy and must continue? Or if it is redundant and can be consolidated with other ministries with the same purpose? Or if it is unnecessary and must be discontinued?

Recruit: What are your criteria in choosing people who can serve in various ministries? How do you assess the character of a candidate for ministry?

Delegate: Do you follow a certain principle in assigning tasks to your coworkers? How can you avoid causing some of your coworkers to be overworked? Do you follow certain principles in allocating budget for various ministries? How do you make plans for the various church ministries?

Envision: As you dream about the ministry and direction of the local church where you serve, how can you assess whether the vision is reasonable, doable, or consistent with God's vision for the church? How can you tell if it is unrealistic, capricious, or incompatible with God's principles?

Respond: How can you distinguish between problems that require long-term solution and those that require short-term solution?

10

The Pastor as a Family Person

A minister's family relates more to his or her profession than normally occurs with any other professions.[1]

—Dennis W. Bickers

PAUL MADE CLEAR HIS expectations from an overseer, "He must manage his own household well, with all dignity keeping his children submissive, for if someone does not know how to manage his own household, how will he care for God's church?" (1 Tim 3:4–5). The ability of the elders to manage the church is gauged by their ability to manage their own family. We have discussed the elder's role as manager of the church in the previous chapter. In this chapter, we will discuss their role as a manager of their own household.

Pastors must not sacrifice their family for ministry. It is true that ministry requires sacrifices, and the family members of the pastor must also be willing to make some sacrifices, too. However, pastors must keep in mind that his family is also part of his ministry. No wonder Paul mentioned household management as part of the requirements for elders. The pastor, therefore, must be a family person who does what is RIGHT. The pastors must see that caring for their family is a Responsibility, it is a divine

1. Bickers, *The Healthy Pastor*, 12.

Imperative, it is Good, it is Healthy, and being a family person is part of the pastor's Testimony.

A FAMILY PERSON DOES WHAT IS RIGHT

Responsibility

"Family," as Asians define it, does not only include spouse and children, but also parents and siblings, even grandparents, uncles, aunts, cousins, and in-laws. In some parts of Asia, the responsibility of caring for the family and extended family falls on one person only. This is clearly unhealthy and not consistent with the Scripture's vision for the family. However, the Scripture provides principles and examples of those who took the responsibility to care for family members who cannot or who can no longer take care of themselves.

The pastor's family must not be sacrificed like a burnt offering, so that its aroma and ashes can cover up the stink of false spirituality and the dirt of irresponsibility. It is true that the cost Jesus demanded from his disciples is high and there are times when the disciple must choose between Christ and family, but he did not call his disciples to abandon their family when they can have both. The fact that the Scripture contains a number of versions of the household code shows that God desires the family to be serving together. Why then did Jesus say, "If anyone comes to me and does not hate his own father and mother and wife and children and brothers and sisters, yes, and even his own life, he cannot be my disciple" (Luke 14:26)? There are situations wherein the family of the disciples *is* the hindrance to their commitment to Christ. In cases like this, the disciples were made to choose between serving God even if they will be persecuted by the family or abandoning God for the sake of family harmony. No wonder Jesus also said, "Do not think that I have come to bring peace to the earth. I have not come to bring peace, but a sword" (Matt 10:34), because the disciple's "enemies" (those who prevent them from making a commitment to God) are members of their family (10:35–37). Nowhere in the Scripture does it teach that the disciples should abandon their family if they are not hindering their commitment to follow Christ.

The story of Jesus's crucifixion is the story of redemption; but there is one incident that shows us the importance of family. Jesus is an example of one who still thought about his mother even at the brink of death, "When Jesus saw his mother and the disciple whom he loved standing nearby, he said to his mother, 'Woman, behold, your son!' Then he said to the disciple,

'Behold, your mother!' And from that hour the disciple took her to his own home" (John 19:26–27). Jesus did not worry about his brothers presumably because they should be able to take care of themselves. As he fulfilled his role as the savior of the world, he was also fulfilling his role as the son of his widowed mother. In ancient Mediterranean society, widows are not like widows today who can be independent, find a job to provide for themselves. Like other widows, Mary needed someone who can take care of her. No wonder Jesus entrusted her mother to one of his disciples who took her home to care for her.

A similar theme is found in Paul's first letter to Timothy. Paul instructed Timothy concerning the widows in the church. It seems that in the first century, there are many widows who needed help, and while the Christian churches were willing to care for their widows, the needs of the widows are greater than the capacity of the churches to provide for them. So Paul advised Timothy to classify the widows into three categories: (1) those who still have family members who can care for them, (2) those who are still young and can remarry, and (3) those who are too old to remarry and without family members to care for them (5:3–16). The church should only be responsible for the third kind.

Concerning those who belong to the first category, Paul said, "But if anyone does not provide for his relatives, and especially for members of his household, he has denied the faith and is worse than an unbeliever" (5:8). The context requires us to interpret the "relatives" and "members of his household" as a reference to the believer's widowed mother or grandmother. Of course, Paul stated a general principle applicable especially for the spouse and children. The phrase "worse than an unbeliever" suggests that Paul expects the believers to be responsible in taking care of their family. Pastors are not exempted from this principle.

Imperative

There is another reason the pastors must manage their family—it is a command. It is a divine imperative that pastors be able to lead or manage their families. One's ability to manage or lead the church is gauged by the person's ability to lead the family (3:4–5). The fact that Paul even included household management as part of the pastor's qualification only shows that for him, the pastor's family plays an important role in the ministry. The pastor's family can either be a help or a hindrance, a support group or a stumbling block, a bulwark or a burden. Thus, it is necessary for pastors to lead their family so that they can serve God together.

The family life and leadership of Joshua suggest a correlation between household management and church management. Not much was said about Joshua's wife and children in the first twenty-three chapters of the book of Joshua. The only time he mentioned about his family was during his final challenge to the Israelites, "And if it is evil in your eyes to serve the LORD, choose this day whom you will serve, whether the gods your fathers served in the region beyond the River, or the gods of the Amorites in whose land you dwell. *But as for me and my house, we will serve the LORD*" (Josh 24:15, italics added). Joshua's leadership in his household translates to his leadership of the nation, "Israel served the LORD all the days of Joshua" (24:31; Judg 2:7). The book of Judges shows what happened after the death of Joshua and the elders who outlived him, "Everyone did what was right in his own eyes" (17:6; 21:25).

In the case of Joshua, we can see that good spiritual leadership in the family is related to good spiritual leadership of the nation, and in the case of the pastors, spiritual leadership in the church. Likewise, poor spiritual leadership in the family is correlated to poor leadership of the nation, as in the case of the priest Eli. The Scripture tells us that Eli had two corrupt sons who served as priests. Despite Eli's reprimand, they refused to listen to their father (1 Sam 2:22–25), and in contrast to the two, "the boy Samuel continued to grow both in stature and in favor with the LORD and also with man" (2:26). It seems odd that while Eli was the priest, God chose not to reveal his plans to Eli, instead he spoke to another prophet (2:27–36) and to the boy Samuel (3:1–4).

Good parenting does not guarantee good children, and poor parenting does not always result in children behaving badly; but we cannot ignore the fact that spiritual leadership within the family is essential to help children grow up to be obedient and with dignity (1 Tim 3:4). On the part of the pastors, they must take seriously the biblical mandate to every believer to lead and care for their family, and to make sure they do not neglect their family for the sake of ministry. Of course, it follows that the pastors must also not use their family as an excuse to neglect their ministry.

On the part of the congregation, they must also take seriously the command to honor those who labor for them, not to immediately believe every accusation against them, but to be bold to correct those who do wrong (5:17, 19–20). Paul's instructions imply that the church must have reasonable expectations from their elders/pastors. One of the challenges the pastors have to face is the extremely high and often unrealistic expectations the congregation places on them and their family. Pastors cannot make mistake, ready to say *yes* to any and every request of the members, and ready to suffer any form of hardships in the ministry including those imposed by church members; and the ministers are not allowed to complain about these. The pastor's wife is often the unpaid staff who is expected to be on-call 24/7, has the musical talent to play instruments or lead the congregation in singing and the ability to teach Sunday school for kids any time they are needed; and like their minister husband, the wife is not allowed to complain about it. The pastor's kids are to behave well, be more mature for their age, and be ready to serve any time they are called to serve; and like their parents, they are not allowed to complain about it. These are, obviously, unrealistic expectations placed on the pastors and their family. This is a reality that pastors must be ready to face, but these challenges should not distract the pastors from the Scripture's expectation that pastors must manage their family.

Good

Managing the family is part of the pastor's responsibility. It is imperative for them to do so. Note, however, that the principles of an orderly family are not just something taught in the Scripture. In fact, every culture has a standard for an orderly family.

More than one version of the household code can be found in the New Testament. Paul listed these codes twice in his letters (Eph 5:22–6:9; Col 3:18–4:1), and Peter has his version of it as well (1 Pet 2:13–3:7). Many other passages in the New Testament also reflect the ideals of the household code. The household code in the New Testament includes various kinds of relationships; husband and wife, parents and children, and masters and slaves. The principle of humble submission to authority and proper exercise of authority, respect and gentle treatment of the other members of the household, and mutual love and care form the basic core of these household codes. Following these principles is good not only for the church, but for the greater society as well.

The Romans also have their picture of the idyllic household. As the household (the smaller units of the society) follow the principles and meet the expectations of an orderly household, the result is a peaceful society. The same principle applies to the church. As the Christian households (the smaller units within the household of God) follow the principles and meet the expectations of a godly household, we can expect to see a healthy church. This means that pastors are not the only ones who are expected to exercise spiritual leadership within their family, but every head of the Christian household must do so. However, those in church leadership are to set an example of spiritual leadership in the household.

Maintaining a healthy marriage is one of the things a married pastor must not neglect, and this requires the pastors to identify the causes of stress in their marriage and to find ways to cope with these stressors. Studies show that spouses of pastors, especially wives of male pastors, are prone to get stressed for the following reasons:

> [Lack] of boundaries between family and work, 'fishbowl' existence, inadequate finances, pressure/expectations from congregation and community to fulfill idealized roles, loss of personal identity, loss of control over personal living environment, adjustment to frequent moves, anger, perception of being second class, lack of tangible results of work, loneliness, lack of social support, work related time demands, unwelcome surprises, routine absence of spouse/father, lack of parallel growth, lack of spiritual care, and psychological disturbances.[2]

Those who participated in these studies show that they found ways of coping with stress, such as spiritual devotion, hobbies, and vacation, among others.[3] Maintaining a healthy marriage takes effort, and pastors must exert effort to achieve it not only because of societal expectations but primarily because a healthy family is consistent with God's design.

The same can be said about the pastor's children. There may be benefits for being a pastor's kid, but the children of ministers also go through stress because of the many expectations some members of the congregation impose on them. They share similar struggles with other kids, such as lack of time spent with their parents, the challenges in school, and problems with friends, among others; but there is a problem that seems to be unique for pastor's kids, and that is the unrealistic expectations placed on them by some church members. This is why church members need to be reminded that every person goes through the various stages of development, even the children of pastors.

Proper household management remains a requirement for those in the ministry. A proper management of the household is necessary to have children that are "obedient" and "with dignity" (1 Tim 3:4), according to Paul. His description of obedience is "with dignity," an expression which can be construed as being beyond the ordinary in the aspect of obedience, and at the same time, it implies a humble obedience without unnecessary humiliation. In practice, this requires the right amount and form of discipline so that the children will obey with joy in their hearts and to do so "with dignity." This is good, not only for the pastors and their children, but also for the congregation as well.

---

2. McMinn, et al., "Care for Pastors," 564.
3. McMinn, et al., "Care for Pastors," 565–67.

Healthy

Proper household management promotes a healthy family. How the pastors raise their children is an essential part of the household management. The pastor's relationship with their spouse also needs to be healthy. The Scripture provides us with direct teachings and several examples to show that relationship of God's servants with their spouse affects their relationship with God, and poor relationship with their spouse may hinder their service to God.

Solomon's marriages are clear examples of how one's spouse can affect both the person's relationship with God and service to him (1 Kgs 11:1–3). In the case of Solomon, his wives's disobedience to God resulted in his disobedience to God. There are cases when God's servants did not succumb to the spouse's pressures. Jezebel's idolatry led Ahab to idolatry (16:31), but Michal's mockery of David's method of worship did not keep him from worshipping God (2 Sam 6:20–23).

The problem of not having a spouse that shares the same faith with the pastor may not be a common problem among pastors. However, in the ministry, pastors who have spouses who do not share the same ministry direction may lead to a lack of support from the spouse and may add unnecessary burden for the pastor to carry. McMinn points out how important is it for male pastors to have a support group other than their wife, "A male pastor relying on his wife for support may function well most of the time, but this narrow support system will become a problem if she is not able to fulfill that role (if she herself becomes burned out, depressed, disabled, disillusioned, and so on)."[4] Yet ministry would be more difficult if the pastor's spouse is not supportive of the pastor's ministry. This applies for female pastors as well. The starting point in dealing with unsupportive spouses is to identify the reasons that makes them unenthusiastic about the pastor's desires or aspirations for the ministry. There may be cases when the spouse simply needs to learn to trust the pastor's decision on how God is leading them, yet there will be instances when the pastor needs to be considerate toward their spouse, understanding their needs, and helping them overcome their fears, anxiety, insecurities, and doubts.

Peter's command to the husbands and wives show how important it is to have order within the family (1 Pet 3:1–7). The wives are instructed to submit to their husbands but the husbands have the responsibility to be considerate toward their wife. Peter made clear that the husband's inconsideration toward their wife is a hindrance to their prayers, "Likewise, husbands, live with your wives in an understanding way, showing honor to

---

4. McMinn, et al., "Care for Pastors," 578.

the woman as the weaker vessel, since they are heirs with you of the grace of life, so that your prayers may not be hindered" (3:7). For pastors especially, hindered prayers mean ineffective ministry.

Pastors may encounter various hindrances in the ministry; some may be caused by the non-believing community that surround them, some by influential leaders of the local church or denomination, but some may be caused by the pastor's family members. This is why building a healthy family is essential for effective ministry.

Testimony

Another variant of the household code in the New Testament is found in Paul's letter to Titus (Tit 2:1–10). Just like the other versions of the household code, there are commands to those with lesser authority (younger ones) to submit to those with greater authority (older ones), and for the latter to teach/train the former. Paul, however, mentioned something important here which he did not discuss in his other letters. He advised the older women to teach the younger ones "to love their husbands and children, to be self-controlled, pure, working at home, kind, and submissive to their own husbands, *that the word of God may not be reviled*" (Tit 2:4–5, italics added).

Paul's statement implies that one of the consequences of having a disorderly family is a bad reputation for the word of God. Conversely, the results of having an orderly household is a good testimony for the word of God. People who adhere to a certain faith are expected to practice the teachings of their religion; or to put it in another way, one's practice reflects the teaching of one's religion. Although this may not be absolutely true, but this is clearly the underlying assumption in Paul's statement. Thus, when a person does something unacceptable in the eyes of the people in their society, the society naturally points to the person's religious teachings as the cause of such practice. In the case of the followers of Jesus who point to the Scripture as their source of authority, when they do something that *unnecessarily* cause the larger society to question their beliefs, the word of God is naturally maligned and blamed.

There will be instances when the beliefs and practices of the Christians do not coincide with norms of the society. When they are slandered because of their beliefs, there is really nothing the believers can do about it. However, there will be instances when the expectations of the society are consistent with the teachings of the Scripture. When Christians are maligned because they failed to meet these expectations, the word of God is maligned with them. As we have mentioned above, even the non-believing Romans have their set of standards for an orderly family. There are lots of similarities between the Scripture's teaching about the household and the ancient Roman societal norms. Paul advocated for an orderly family, not only because it is right and it pleases God, but it also brings honor to the word of God. It is part of the Christian's testimony to the world that the God we serve is the God of order. Pastors are no exceptions. As they manage their family and promote order, they testify of the same thing and give no legitimate reason for non-believers to revile the word of God. Andreas J. Köstenberger and David W. Jones explain one of the motivations of the household codes in the New Testament, "Marriage, as well as other human relationships, is thus set in the larger framework of a believer's Christian testimony in the surrounding unbelieving world."[5]

Of course, the pastors who set their family in order do not only testify before the unbelieving world, they also set an example for the members of the congregation. On the brighter side, most members of the congregation look at the family of the pastor, not for the purpose of finding something to criticize, but because they are looking for models of family to imitate. This does not really take the pressure off the shoulders of the pastors and their family, but this seems to be the preferable option as long as the pastors and their family do not feel the need to give an impression of perfection and they are willing to admit that they share the same struggles every family experience.

If the families within the church look to the pastor's family for inspiration and example of household management, where can the pastors look for inspiration and example? Pastors should not make the mistake of thinking that they *always* have to assume the role of the exemplar. There will be many instances when they, too, will benefit from learning from godly members within the congregation on how to manage the household. In fact, there are so much that the pastors can learn from the flock, and household management is one of them.

THE PASTOR AS A FAMILY PERSON

Pastors are called to manage the household of God, but as Paul made clear, the way they manage their own family is indicative of how they will manage the church. Household management is one of Paul's requirements from an elder/pastor. The Scripture never require the pastor to sacrifice their family for the sake of ministry. The only time Jesus required his disciples to choose between him or their family is when the family is preventing the disciples from following him.

5. Köstenberger and Jones, *God, Marriage, and Family*, 53.

The family of the pastors is an essential part of their ministry. Thus, the pastor must aim to be a family person because it is RIGHT.

- Responsibility: Pastors are not exempted from the believer's responsibility to care for their family, especially for those who cannot care for themselves.
- Imperative: The Scripture commands the believers, pastors included, to manage their household well.
- Good: Managing the household is a good thing. Even those who do not follow the teachings of Jesus will agree.
- Healthy: There may be things that hinder the pastors from managing their household. They must take time to identify and deal with these hindrances.
- Testimony: By managing their household well, the pastors testify of the work of God in their lives before the non-believers and set an example for believers to follow.

Questions for Personal Reflection

Responsibility: Is Paul's command to care for family members *merely* cultural? What are the implications of your answer?

Imperative: What do you think is the greatest challenge we face in raising children today? What can we do to overcome this difficulty?

Good: Considering the context where you serve, what are some practices and expectations relating to family that are consistent with the Scripture's teachings? What are some that are inconsistent with the Scripture's standard?

Healthy: What are some of the hindrances you are encountering in the ministry? What are their causes? How can you develop a healthy relationship with your family members?

Testimony: As a pastor, how can you encourage your family members to take up the challenge of setting an example for the other families in the church without being stressed out? How can you help your family cope with the stress of "living in a fishbowl"?

11

The Pastor as a Liturgist

Few privileges are greater than leading Christians in their worship of God. It may be from a pulpit or a platform; it may be to a large congregation or a house group. We often shrink beforehand at the awesome responsibility, and yet find great joy in fulfilling it.[1]

—Derek J. Prime and Alistair Begg

The roles we have discussed so far show that there are various ministries in which the pastors can be involved, but these ministries are not equally visible. Perhaps the ministry that makes pastors most visible is their work as the worship leader. When I say "worship leader," I am not referring to the one who leads the congregation in singing (as the expression is often used today), but as one who leads the whole congregation in worship. His preaching ministry in the church is only a part of his work as the liturgist who leads the whole congregation in worship.

As the liturgist, the pastors must show God's WORTH to the congregation. This begins with pastors who Worship God, who ensure Order in worship, make sure the people understood the meaning of the Rites, lead the congregation in Thanksgiving, and exhort them through the Homilies.

---

1. Prime and Begg, *On Being a Pastor*, 188.

LITURGISTS SHOW GOD'S WORTH

Worship

Worship is not just what we do every first day of the week in the sanctuary or worship hall; it is how we live our life the rest of the week (Rom 12:1-2). Worshipping God with our life is vital. More so, the pastors who lead the worship must be careful not to forget this truth because only a worshipper can truly lead others in worship.

The early Christians began a new tradition by meeting every first day of the week which is Sunday (Acts 20:7), in addition to their regular meetings on the last day of the week or the Sabbath. However, more important than their weekly meetings is the life they live during the rest of the week. Luke provides us with a picture of an early community of worshippers (2:42-47). We are told that the believers "devoted themselves to the apostles' teaching and the fellowship, to the breaking of bread and the prayers" (2:42). They were devoted to the point that they met regularly; and in their case, "regular" means "day by day" (2:46). More important than their regular meetings is how they live as a community. The church in Jerusalem was not affluent. In several instances in Paul's letters, he mentioned about the collection he made from the other churches so that he can bring some financial relief for the Jerusalem church (Rom 15:26-28; 1 Cor 16:1-2). Given their condition, the members who owned properties sold what they have in order to share with those who have less (Acts 2:44-45). This was their "spiritual act of worship" (Rom 12:2). Every believer is expected to live the life of a worshipper, and pastors are not exempted.

Worship is not only something one does when times are good. Even in difficult times, the worshipper continues to worship. When Paul and Silas were imprisoned, they were worshiping when an earthquake left the prison doors opened (Acts 16:25-26). The jailer almost took his life, not because he was awestruck after seeing God's miraculous work, but because he knew he would be held accountable even if only one of the prisoners escaped (16:27). The fact that Paul and other prisoners did not escape even though they have the opportunity to do so opened the opportunity for Paul to preach to the jailer (16:32). God's miraculous work shows that he is indeed worthy of worship. As God's servants worship him even through adversities, his work continued to grow and more people became worshippers (16:30-34).

One of the most challenging parts of being a pastor is dealing with false accusations. There are three kinds of people in the congregation. First, those who have the moral courage to honestly and lovingly tell the pastors if the latter make mistakes, and they do so without malicious intent. This is the best type of member, and they are rare. Unfortunately, there is a second group who overlook every wrong done by the pastor, whether out of respect for the office, for fear of authority, for feeling of unworthiness to point out the pastor's mistake, or for other reasons. Among these we can find some who are worshippers of the pastor. In the third group are those who enjoy scrutinizing the pastors, finding every mistake they make often resulting in gossips, slander, and false accusations against the pastors. Among these three, only the first one is desirable. Oden has some advice for pastors under attack.

> When ministry is under unjust attack by those who would seek to discredit it, it is fitting to respond proportionally in a way that is consistent with everything else that the care of souls stands for. This may require astute efforts to preserve the community from devisiveness. From Jesus' ministry to the present, the care of souls has had to deal with serious challenges from determined detractors. Nothing is more salutary, under such circumstances, than to reflect fundamentally upon the nature of the church as a redemptive community.[2]

He further explains, "False accusations against the pastor are best answered through a life lived in congruence with one's teachings."[3] The pastors who speak against pride will be asked if they are humble; those who teach about purity will be subject to test whether they are pure; and those who preach against avarice will have their lifestyle checked. The pastors who worship God with their life need not fear malicious people because their way of life is their best defense. This is the first step in leading the people to a life of worship.

Order

Every Christian tradition has its own order of worship. Although there are some variations in the order of worship among these traditions, the ways they conduct worship services remain comparable. Worship services typically include prayers and benediction, sermons, songs, and communion. In some churches, sharing of testimonies, and even baptism, are also part of the worship service.

The order of worship or the sequence of the program usually depends on the church's tradition. The Bible does not give us a template on how to

2. Oden, *Classical Pastoral Care*, 2:216–17.
3. Oden, *Classical Pastoral Care*, 2:217.

arrange the program for the worship service. Thus, in some sense, there is no right or wrong when we talk about the sequence of the program provided it does not include anything that takes our focus away from God to something else. The pastor as a liturgist must decide the best sequence for the program, what should or should not be included, and what may or may not be included.

More important than the order of worship is the rationale behind every element of the worship service. Paul L. Homer explains,

> To worship God requires that one really worship him and not get engrossed in the liturgy. The liturgy gets its legitimacy and point from the fact that God requires an offering, enjoins contrition and repentance, promises a pardon, and proffers redemption. But this makes sense only because there is a God whose will is our law, whose pardon is our renewed life, and whose mercy reads our very hearts.[4]

When we live our life in obedience to God, this is the Christian's "spiritual act of worship" (Rom 12:1). Essential to a life of obedience is participation in corporate worship. Individual worship and corporate worship are intricately joined. The same God who required the Israelites to live a life of obedience is the same God who required them to offer various sacrifices. The same God whose words are read by the Jews every Sabbath is also the same God who expected them to obey. The same God to whom the Christians pray when they meet together is the same God who demanded obedience from them. The same God who should be at the center of the life of individual worshippers is the same God who should be at the center of corporate worship.

Since *the object of worship is the God who demands obedience*, we cannot worship him any way we wanted. No wonder God drew boundaries for Israel as to what can or cannot be done whenever they come to God in worship (Deut 12:29–32). Likewise, the God who demands obedience must be worshipped in a way that pleases him, therefore, nothing that displeases him must be done in the worship service. Moreover, since *God should be at the center of every worship service*, anything that takes the focus of the worshippers away from God must be removed.

God is worthy of worship. Thus, it is just right for the one who leads the worship to ensure a smooth and orderly worship. Paul's first letter to the Corinthians shows an example of how a worship service can be disorderly. He set a clear principle for an orderly worship, "What then, brothers? When you come together, each one has a hymn, a lesson, a revelation, a tongue, or an interpretation. Let all things be done for building up" (1 Cor 14:26). The

---

4. Homer, "About Liturgy and Its Logic," 21.

purpose of a worship service is to glorify God, and the way to glorify God during the worship service is by edifying God's people. *An orderly worship must be designed to build up the body of believers.* For this reason, those who serve must use their spiritual gifts with this as their only purpose.

The use of spiritual gifts must contribute to the edification of the believers. In the case of the Corinthians, the use of their gifts had become disruptive at some points. Paul's instructions to limit the number of those who speak in tongues, to do so only if there is an interpreter, and to take turns in speaking (14:27–30) were not intended to prohibit the use of spiritual gifts but to ensure an orderly worship; as he said, "For God is not a God of confusion but of peace" (14:33). The purpose of the worship service is not to showcase the gifts and abilities of any individual, whether it is the preacher, the song leader or choir, or anyone involved in any program. Everyone who serves during the worship service is expected to give his or her best, yet the focus of the service is still to glorify God by edifying God's people.

Rites

Rituals are integral part of worship. They do not only symbolize certain scriptural truths, but they can also be a channel through which God bestows his blessings upon his people. Rituals, however, can also become empty practices; and this happens if we do them regularly without asking why we do them.

Christian churches, regardless of the denominations, have considered baptism and communion as essential practices of the Christian faith. For the one being baptized, baptism is an expression of repentance. John's baptism is thus described, "John appeared, baptizing in the wilderness and proclaiming a baptism of repentance for the forgiveness of sins" (Mark 1:4; see also Luke 3:3). Peter preached to the Diaspora Jews telling them to be baptized as expression of their repentance, "And Peter said to them, 'Repent and be baptized every one of you in the name of Jesus Christ for the forgiveness of your sins, and you will receive the gift of the Holy Spirit'" (Acts 2:38). Baptism is not only an expression of repentance, but it is also an expression of faith. Thus, Jesus commissioned his disciples to preach and baptize (Mark 16:15–16). As water is normally used for cleansing, baptism is also a symbol of the cleansing of sins. So when Ananias prayed for the restoration of Paul's sight, he also encouraged Paul to be baptized (Acts 22:16). Baptism is a ritual of incorporating new members into the body, just like the Gentiles who were baptized were publicly recognized as members of one community together with the Jews. Thus, Peter wasted no time challenging Cornelius, together with his friends and relatives, to be baptized (10:47–48). In this way, baptism is a testimony of unity of the believers within one body of Christ.

Since baptism carries a rich meaning, baptism should not be seen as a mere ritual but as an essential part of pastoral care, so that as the pastor baptizes the believers, the latter will be reminded that their sins are cleansed and they are incorporated into the body of Christ. As Oden also explains,

> Care of souls precedes baptism in one sense, for much that the pastor does leads to baptism. Yet in another sense, the care of souls within the Christian community begins with baptism. For in baptism new life in the caring community is visibly manifested. Baptism marks a starting point in the care of a particular person within the community of faith. The personal name traditionally given in baptism marks the receiving of an identity within the healing, redemptive family of God.[5]

The Lord's Supper or the Communion is also an important part of community worship. About two decades after Jesus's resurrection, Paul was already talking about the Lord's Supper as a tradition that was handed down by Jesus through the apostles and early believers, "For I received from the Lord what I also delivered to you" (1 Cor 11:23a). This is something believers do regularly when they meet (11:20). As Paul explained, this practice was done in obedience to Jesus's command to remember him (11:24–25; Luke 22:19). As a sacred ritual, this cannot be done in an unworthy manner (1 Cor 11:27). This is the reason why it is important to incorporate a time, albeit brief, for the believer to examine themselves and confess their sins prior to the distribution of the elements. Again, Oden points out, "As nature provides animals with remedies for injury, so does grace provide the wounded human soul the remedy of confession (*exomologesis*) and communion."[6] Participating in the communion is a good opportunity to be reminded that our sins are forgiven and cleansed because of the body of Jesus was broken and his blood was shed; and it is the duty of pastors as the liturgist to remind the congregation of this valuable truth.

Mutual respect is necessary as different denominations may administer baptism and communion differently. Rituals have their function. Forms may change or vary, functions do not.

---

5. Oden, *Classical Pastoral Care*, 2:217.
6. Oden, *Classical Pastoral Care*, 2:136.

Thanksgiving

Public prayers were part of the religious gathering of the ancient Jews. This is one of the things Christians learned from the Jews, aside from the public reading of Scripture. We have several examples from the Scripture of corporate prayers showing the various reasons why the Jews pray publicly and as a community.

First, confession of sins was part of corporate prayers. Ezra led the Jews who returned from Babylon to spiritual renewal by admitting that their exile was a consequence of their disobedience to God's commands (Ezra 10:1). Second, praises and thanksgivings were also part of the corporate prayers of the Jews. A number of psalms can be cited as examples (22:22; 35:18; 40:10; 68:26; 107:32; 149:1). One of them is Psalm 111 where the worship leader declares, "Praise the Lord! I will give thanks to the Lord with my whole heart, in the company of the upright, in the congregation" (111:1). Third, public prayers can also be done to present petitions to God corporately. Asaph, for instance, led the assembly to pray for God's vindication (74:2). Fourth, the benediction is also an integral part of the religious assembly. God instructed Moses to tell Aaron to bless the congregation by saying, "The Lord bless you and keep you; the Lord make his face to shine upon you and be gracious to you; the Lord lift up his countenance upon you and give you peace" (Num 16:22–27). With this instruction is God's promise to indeed bless the congregation.

These are the elements that can be included in pastoral prayers. First, pastors should lead the congregation in a prayer of confession especially for national sins or known sins committed by members of the congregation. Confession is an inevitable step to human's restoration to God. Corporate confessions are constant reminders to the congregation that they need to regularly examine themselves to see if there is anything that hinders their relationship with God. Second, as pastors lead the congregation in prayers of praise, the congregation is reminded about the character and works of the God they serve. Third, prayers of petition are reminders of our need for God. There are so many things that can be included in our petitions to God. James instructed the believers to ask the elders of the congregation to pray for those who are sick (Jas 5:14). This can be done both in the homes of the sick person, and even during worship services so that the congregation can be involved in praying for those who are struggling with their health. There are instructions in the Scripture to pray for those in authority; not only because their decisions can affect the lives of the people, but also because it is something that pleases God (1 Tim 2:1–4). Finally, a pronouncement of blessing is also appropriate considering God's promise to bless his people through the blessing of his servant. All these must include thanksgiving: for God's forgiveness, for the work God is doing, for God's answer to our prayers, and for God's continuous blessings.

The pastors as liturgist must lead the congregation in worship through prayer, but pastors must be careful not to propagate the unspoken superstition of many believers that only pastoral prayers are effective. It is true that when James said, "The prayer of a righteous person has great power as it is working" (Jas 5:16), he was referring to the elders who pray for those in need. He was not in any way suggesting that *only* pastors are the "righteous person" whose prayers are heard by God. The congregation must be encouraged to pray publicly. Dale Patrick and James Kratz address another problem related to the lack of participation of the congregation in prayer. They point out the differences between churches that use the formal prayer printed either on the program sheets or hymnals/prayer books that the congregation can read and those churches that prefer spontaneous prayer. The danger of being dry and wooden is real for churches that use the formal method of public prayer, but those who practice spontaneous prayers are not really exempt from the same kind of dryness brought by repeating stock phrases often used in public prayers.[7] The problem of senseless and repetitive prayers was already addressed by Jesus (Matt 6:5–8). The key is to be constantly aware of our natural tendency to do things perfunctorily and remind ourselves to avoid it every time we pray publicly. Moreover, it is important to get the congregation to participate in public prayer. Patrick and Kratz suggest some practical steps to do so: (1) inform the congregation items that they can pray about; (2) invite them to share their personal thanksgivings and petitions; and (3) set a time for the congregation to pray with one another during the worship service.[8]

Homilies

The New Testament provides hints that aside from baptism and communion, other practices were included as part of their corporate worship. For instance, Paul encouraged Timothy to continue with the public reading of the Scripture to go together with exhortation and teaching (1 Tim 4:13). This is especially important in an oral and aural society, wherein people learn the Scripture more by hearing it read than by personally reading it. No wonder John also expects the book of Revelation be read publicly by one person while the rest listens (Rev 1:3).

---

7. Patrick and Kratz, "Act of the Congregation," 186–87.
8. Patrick and Kratz, "Act of the Congregation," 188.

Believers today no longer read from scrolls like the ancient believers. The codex, which was an innovation a couple of centuries after Jesus and had become the prototype for modern books, is slowly being replaced by newer innovations in the modern era, the electronic Bibles. The use of printed Bibles or electronic Bibles is a matter of preference, not to be an issue of spirituality. Although times have changed and will continue to change, and there are more people who can read for themselves, it does not diminish the importance of this practice because public reading of Scripture is an essential part of exhortation and teaching. The public reading of Scripture was not a practice introduced by Christians. It had been practiced by Jews as they meet in the synagogues during Sabbath. Jesus participated in corporate worship by reading the Scripture publicly, "And he came to Nazareth, where he had been brought up. And as was his custom, he went to the synagogue on the Sabbath day, and he stood up to read" (Luke 4:16). He did not just read the words of Isaiah, but he also explained what it means.

Aside from the public reading of Scripture and prayer, the Christian's practice of sharing words of exhortation finds its precedent in the ancient synagogue meetings of the Jews. Paul preached in one of these meetings in Antioch of Syria, "After the reading from the Law and the Prophets, the rulers of the synagogue sent a message to them, saying, 'Brothers, if you have any word of encouragement for the people, say it'" (Acts 13:15). For the Jews, the Law of Moses is central in their preaching (15:21). For the Christians, Sunday worship services focus on the person, teachings, and work of Jesus.

Ezra provided a good example for preachers to follow by showing the important elements of a homily, "For Ezra had set his heart to *study* the Law of the LORD, and to *do* it and to *teach* his statutes and rules in Israel." (Ezra 7:10, italics added). First, he set his heart *to study the Law of the LORD*. Pastors should not take their sermons lightly. For a seminarian training to become a pastor, behind a 30-minute sermon could 30-hour preparation. As the pastor continue to study the word, the number of hours for preparing a sermon may decrease. Nonetheless, every sermon still requires careful preparation. The pastors as liturgists must be dedicated and aim to be like Ezra "who set his heart to study" the word of God.

Second, Ezra also set his heart *to do it*. Homilies are not speeches or lectures. Its purpose is to pass on, not just sound information, but also spiritual insights. This means that as the pastor-liturgist prepare sermons to speak to the people, the Scripture must first speak to them. In the first place, pastors are members of God's people, and God's message to God's people is also God's message to them. The pastors must see themselves as members of the believing community to whom God is speaking even though they assume the role of the messenger. As members of God's community, they must also respond in obedience to God's word. This statement may sound like pastors are expected to be perfect first before they can preach; this clearly cannot happen. Pastors/liturgists are not expected to be perfect, but they must respond to God's message the same way the other members of the congregation are expected to respond. The last thing we want Jesus to say to the congregation about us is, "do and observe whatever they tell you, but not the works they do. For they preach, but do not practice" (Matt 23:2).

Finally, Ezra set his heart to *teach his statutes and rules to Israel*. After studying and practicing God's teachings, the pastors are ready to teach. Preaching is a form of teaching, and teaching is an essential part of preaching. Sometimes, pastors are criticized because "they preach as if they are teaching (lecturing)," or vice versa. Such comment is clearly uncalled for, and arrogant at its core. The comment is actually about the preacher's style of delivery, which must be distinguished from the content of the message; interestingly, the critique implies that preaching and teaching are two different and unrelated things. There is, however, no clear distinction between teaching and preaching in the New Testament. Pastors teach by preaching and they preach for the purpose of teaching, just like what Jesus did, "When Jesus had finished instructing his twelve disciples, he went on from there to teach and preach in their cities" (Matt 11:1; cf. Luke 20:1; Acts 5:42; 15:35). The goal of preaching/teaching is to see people practice the lessons from Scripture. Ezra taught "statutes and rules" to the people, not hifalutin theological concepts that only a few theologians truly understand. Statutes and rules expect practical responses; in other words, whatever Ezra taught, he expected the people to do. Likewise, the liturgist should expect the people to do whatever they teach.

THE PASTOR AS A LITURGIST

Corporate worship is an essential part of the life of the believer. Participation in public worship is a response to one of God's requirement from the believers. It is also a way for the believers to acknowledge God for who he is and what he is doing. Leading the people in corporate worship is one of the responsibilities of the pastor.

As the liturgist, the pastor must show God's WORTH to the congregation.

- Worship: The pastor who leads the congregation must also be a worshipper of God. The pastor's testimony shows that God is worthy of worship.

- Order: The Scripture does not in any way present God as one who is too rigid and inflexible, but this does not mean he does not expect an orderly worship.
- Rites: The pastor as liturgist must constantly remind the congregation why certain rituals are essential to prevent them from forgetting what these rituals mean.
- Thanksgiving: Public prayers and thanksgiving are means to be reminded of the power of God and how he cares for his people.
- Homilies: Through sermons, the pastors can continuously declare the goodness and greatness of God, and invite the congregation to respond to God and participate in what he is doing.

Questions for Personal Reflection

Worship: How can we maintain our walk with God? How can we make sure we respond in humility to the commendations of the members of the congregation? How do we maintain teachability to the fair but negative comments we hear? Where do we get encouragements when there are unfair and slanderous criticisms against us?

Order: How do we ensure that the Sunday worship is orderly? Have you set criteria to help you decide what can or cannot be included as part of the worship service?

Rites: How can you ensure that the congregation understands the meaning of the sacred rites like baptism and communion? What steps can you do to make sure that the congregation does not go through meaningless rituals only?

Thanksgiving: What are some of the unspoken superstitions that some members of the congregation believe about prayer? How can this be corrected? How can you encourage the congregation to participate in public prayer?

Homilies: How can you make sure that the sermons the congregation hear every Sunday brings God glory? How can we make sure that they provide the people with practical and doable steps to live out their faith?

12

The Pastor as a Hermit

> Caring for the flock cannot occur unless one first cares for oneself, watches over one's own welfare, feeds and nurtures one's own body and soul.[1]
>
> —Thomas C. Oden

Considering everything we have discussed up to this point, it is clear that the pastoral ministry is challenging. For this reason, it is important for the pastor to have a regular time to rest and be refreshed. We often refer to this as our "Sabbath day" or weekly "day-off." Of course, as servants there will be occasions when we need to do ministry even on our day-off. There are instances when Jesus had to give up his time of rest to minister to those in need. For instance, when Jesus heard about the death of John the Baptist, he went to a desolate place by himself. The sequence of events suggests that Jesus withdrew to grieve for John, but even in time of grief, when the crowd came to him, he willingly gave up his personal time to minister to them (Matt 14:10–14).

There may be times when the pastor's personal time will be cut short, but it does not diminish the importance of having a time to recharge. Once in a while we need to be like hermits who withdrew from the crowd to

---

1. Oden, *Classical Pastoral Care*, 2:7.

spend extended time together with God. The pastor as hermit RESTS in the Lord. They need time to Refresh, to Examine their heart, for Solitude, to Think, and to develop Sensitivity to God's leading.

A HERMIT RESTS IN THE LORD

Refresh

Pastors are humans, and humans get tired. In short, pastors get tired. There is only one thing a tired person needs to do—rest. Whether it be physical, emotional, or spiritual exhaustion, the only solution for tiredness is rest. There may be times when we are physically tired, but spiritually recharged; and there may be times when we are physically exhausted because we are spiritually or emotionally drained. Our physical body, mind, and emotions are intricately linked. The only way to recover from weariness is rest. As finite humans with limited capacities, there is no way we can be continuously be effective without resting. The only way to consistently move forward is to understand the way God designed humans—as creatures who need to rest. Rudy Dirks talks about the importance of resting, "Sabbath was made for humanity to find its place in God—and since God is the source of life, the sustainer of life, and the very expression of life itself, then resting in God can only be life giving."[2]

The story of Elijah illustrates the importance rest, especially for those in ministry. Elijah's first recorded task was to confront King Ahab of the sins he caused Israel to commit and inform him of God's plan to send drought for an extended period of time as consequence of their idolatry (1 Kgs 16:29–17:1). After the confrontation, Elijah was forced to withdraw and be totally dependent on God's provisions through the ravens (which were considered unclean birds [Lev 11:15]), and through a widow (who was considered helpless in the ancient Jewish society).

The confrontation between Ahab and Elijah resumed a couple of years later which eventually led to an encounter between God's prophet Elijah and the 850 false prophets of Baal and Asherah (1 Kgs 18:1–19). Elijah witnessed spiritual victory (18:20–40), but the battle continued because Ahab's wife Jezebel plotted to kill Elijah and he had to run away (19:1–3), resulting in physical and psychological exhaustion (19:4). His work was not yet over, but God knew exactly what Elijah needed—rest. God blessed him with an opportunity to recharge amidst the chaos. Twice God provided food for him to eat and allowed him to just sleep (19:5–7). With these provisions, Elijah

2. Dirks, "Journey Toward Sabbath Rest," 56.

"went in the strength of that food forty days and forty nights to Horeb, the mount of God" (19:8). God was not finished yet. He did not only help Elijah recover from physical fatigue after running hundreds of kilometers, he also enabled the prophet to regain a proper perspective about his situation (19:9–18). After which, God raised up another prophet to come alongside Elijah as he continued his ministry (19:19–21). Thus, God helped Elijah to recover, not only from physical tiredness, but also from mental, spiritual, and emotional exhaustion.

With renewed strength, Elijah continued his ministry during the reign of Ahab. The final recorded encounter between them was after Ahab abused his power, unlawfully taking Naboth's ancestral property by falsely accusing the latter of blasphemy. Ahab did this upon Jezebel's prompting (21:1–16). Elijah was able to do his ministry the way he did before. Likewise, the pastor must find time to rest when necessary so that they can continue to serve God with renewed strength.

Resting is an admission of human limitations. It is a necessary part of human life to maintain spiritual, physical, mental, and emotional health. Resting should not be equated with laziness. A reasonable amount of rest is a necessary ingredient to efficiency. Continuously working while we are tired only makes us less productive; six days of efficient work have better results than seven days of inefficient work. Resting is not the opposite of diligence; on the contrary, the right amount of rest is part of being diligent. It can sometimes be a motivation to make use of one's time well so as to finish a realistic amount of work within a given period and still have time to recharge. Resting is also a way of acknowledging that it is God who is in control. If pastors think that if they are not around everything will fall apart, they will find it difficult to get the rest they need. This mentality actually shows a deeper problem. Dirks explains, "Sabbath rest teaches us our need to learn to not be in control, to not be responsible for the well-being of everyone else in the church. The Sabbath heart is a heart that is at rest in God. God initiates; we respond."[3]

Examine

The discipline of introspection is important for those in the ministry. God knows what is in our hearts, but we may not always be aware of them (Ps 139:1–6). Like the psalmist, pastors must learn to pray, "Search me, O God, and know my heart! Try me and know my thoughts! And see if there be any grievous way in me, and lead me in the way everlasting!" (139:23–24)

3. Dirks, "Journey Toward Sabbath Rest," 55.

A common alliteration of the three types of temptations pastors constantly face is: glory, gold, and girls/guys. Some vary the alliteration to prestige, power, and pleasure; or others may use fame, fortune, and fantasies. Jesus went through three kinds of temptation also (Matt 4:1–11; Luke 4:1–13); one that has to do with the needs of the physical body (turning stones to bread), one with power and possessions (kingdoms of world), and one with honor (jumping from the top of the temple). John classifies sins into the "the desires of the flesh and the desires of the eyes and pride of life" (1 John 2:16). Sins can easily creep into one's heart. Regularly examining our heart is good because it brings to light what is in it.

In the past few decades, we often hear news about pastors who have been involved in sexual misconduct or in embezzlement. These are serious sins and we cannot take them lightly; but we who hear about this news should heed Paul's reminder, "Keep watch on yourself, lest you too be tempted" (Gal 6:1b). Hence, pastors must constantly examine how they relate with the opposite sex and how they handle finances, lest they fall in these areas. News about pastors who commit sexual sins or have been dishonest with finances are usually sensationalized; these two sins may fall under the first two categories of sins mentioned by John, namely, the lust of the flesh and the lust of the eyes. Interestingly, we seldom talk about the third sin mentioned by John—the pride of life.

Of the three sins mentioned above, pride is the one we take least seriously. This makes introspection even more important for the minister. It is possible to serve with wrong motives like the preachers in Philippi (Phil 1:15), or to desire spiritual gifts for self-glorification like Simon Magus (Acts 8:18–23). Pastors must aim to say like Paul, "So I always take pains to have a clear conscience toward both God and man" (Acts 24:16); and, "For our boast is this, the testimony of our conscience, that we behaved in the world with simplicity and godly sincerity, not by earthly wisdom but by the grace of God, and supremely so toward you" (2 Cor 1:12). Thus, he advised Timothy to aim for a clear conscience (1 Tim 1:5, 19). Pastors should aim for the same; and self-examination is necessary part of the process to reach it.

Too much introspection can be dangerous as well. In C. S. Lewis's classic *Screwtape Letters*, he imagines the correspondences between an expert tempter Uncle Screwtape and his novice nephew Wormwood. In one of Screwtape's letters, as he did in the others, he advises Wormwood how to be effective in tempting a person.

> Keep his mind on the inner life. He thinks his conversion is something *inside* him and his attention is therefore chiefly turned at present to the states of his own mind—or rather to

that very expurgated version of them which is all you should allow him to see. Encourage this. Keep his mind off the most elementary duties by directing it to the most advanced and spiritual ones. Aggravate that most useful human characteristic, the horror and neglect of the obvious. You must bring him to a condition in which he can practice self-examination for an hour without discovering any of those facts about himself which are perfectly clear to anyone who has ever lived in the same house with him or worked in the same office.[4]

The letters are clearly fictional, but the reality it reflects is undeniable. Self-examination is good a spiritual exercise, and introspection is useless without the work of the Spirit in the heart of the pastor. The pastor cannot continue with this exercise without recalling what the prophet Jeremiah said about the human heart, "The heart is deceitful above all things, and desperately sick; who can understand it?" (Jer 17:9). Only the Spirit can bring to light what is in the dark and reveal what is hidden within the recesses of the hearts; and he alone can bring about genuine transformation.

Solitude

Throughout the centuries, Christians practiced various forms of spiritual disciplines. Some take the vow of silence hoping to hear God's voice clearly; others take the vow of celibacy because it is viewed as a means to chastity; still others abstain from certain food because they are considered unclean; and there are those who think that self-flagellations and chanting mantras are good for the soul. Spiritual disciplines can be done either for good or for selfish reasons.

Jesus preached against hypocrisy using three types of spiritual disciplines as illustrations: almsgiving, prayer, and fasting. This suggests that these are the disciplines his contemporaries commonly practiced. His message is against those who practice these disciplines to honor themselves. There is nothing in his sermon to suggest that he was discouraging his followers to practice any of these. On the contrary, he advised his followers to make sure that if they practice these, it should be for the sole purpose of glorifying God.

Aside from these disciplines, Jesus exemplified another form of spiritual discipline, namely, the discipline of solitude. Mark tells us that Jesus rises early to go to a desolate place to pray (Mark 1:35). Ruth Haley Barton describes the positive impact of practicing solitude.

4. Lewis, *The Screwtape Letters*, 11–12.

> Solitude and silence are disciplines that provide us with a place to rest in God and listen to the voice of the One who calls us his beloved in quiet, sure tones. Many of us have been schooled in traditional "quiet time" approaches that often feel like another place of human striving and hard work—even when our activities are as lofty as Bible study, prayer, and journaling. For Christian leaders in particular, it can become hard to distinguish between the work we do *for* God and the time for us to *be with* God, resting in him and enjoying his presence. Scripture can be reduced to a textbook from which we gain information for being successful in ministry and prayer can become an exhausting round of different kinds of mental activity.[5]

Three things are worth noting about Jesus's practice of solitude: (1) he did it before dawn; (2) he did it in a desolate place; and (3) he prayed. First, Jesus rise up early for prayer. Reformers like Martin Luther was also known to habitually rise up early for prayer. There are good reasons why this practice is good. Doing it first thing in the morning prepares the minister for the day ahead. This may not work for everyone, however. Waking up very early in the morning to pray is only one of the forms of this spiritual discipline. In fact, the Scripture contains examples of people who pray in the morning (Ps 5:3); and those who pray in the evening (6:6). The act of prayer is more important than the time of prayer.

Second, Jesus went to a desolate place to pray. The desert fathers have spent much of their time away from people to practice their religious disciplines. There are good reasons why this practice is commendable. This practice is consistent with Jesus's advice to pray in secret (Matt 6:6). Jesus never discouraged public prayer. As we discussed in the chapter on the *Pastor as a Liturgist*, public prayer is a necessary part of corporate worship. Jesus, however, spoke against hypocritical public prayer. Private prayer is a way to nourish one's soul. Also, finding a private space to pray provides the believers freedom from unnecessary distractions. Being free from distractions allow the believer extended time to pray. Again, this is not to suggest that longer prayers are better than short ones. Keep in mind that this is one of the wrong assumptions Jesus tried to correct. Thus, he said, "And when you pray, do not heap up empty phrases as the Gentiles do, for they think that they will be heard for their many words" (6:7). Peter's prayer, "Lord, save me" (14:30), is no less effective than Solomon's prayer of dedication (1 Kgs 8:22–61), or even Jesus's prayer (John 17:1–26). The efficacy of prayer is not based on the one who prays nor on the length of the prayer, but on

---

5. Barton Haley, "It Begins with You," 32.

the one who listens to the prayer. The key principle for the pastors is to find a place wherein they can be free from distractions in order to have an extended time to be alone with God.

Third, Jesus prayed. More important than the place and time is the act prayer. Prayer is an expression of dependence upon God, regardless of the place or time or length of time it was done. The pastors must be constantly dependent upon God's strength, and times of solitude is a necessity in the ministry.

Think

According to Jesus, the greatest commandment is this, "You shall love the Lord your God with all your heart and with all your soul and *with all your mind*" (Matt 22:37, italics added). Christian spirituality is incomplete if we neglect the mind. While it is true that having information from the Scripture is not the same as having insights from the Scripture, and that there is a difference between knowledge and wisdom, we must not forget that the ability to acquire knowledge and information, and the capacity to gain wisdom and spiritual insight both come from God.

Paul stressed the importance of the mind several times in his letters. He pointed out the need to set our mind on the Spirit (Rom 8:6–7). The renewal of the mind is the key so that the believers will not be conformed to the patterns of this world (12:2). He also stressed the need to have the "mind of Christ" (1 Cor 2:16); and also, the perils of being "alienated and hostile in mind" (Col 1:21), because having a depraved mind only results in ungodliness (1 Tim 6:5). Even spiritual disciplines like prayer involves the mind, so he says, "What am I to do? I will pray with my spirit, but I will pray with my mind also; I will sing praise with my spirit, but I will sing with my mind also" (1 Cor 14:15). The mind can be used to dishonor God, but it can also be used to glorify the one who created it. Christian spirituality must not be devoid of its use, and the extended time the pastors spend with God is a good time for them to do some reflections.

Paul's letters include several biographical sections where he recounted his travels, his ministries, and even the challenges he encountered. In his letter to the Galatians, he told the believers that after his encounter with the risen Christ and before he started preaching the message of resurrection to the Gentiles, instead of consulting the apostles immediately, he recalled, "I went away into Arabia, and returned again to Damascus" (Gal 1:17). He did not specify what he did in the desert of Arabia, nor did he tell the Galatians what he did in Damascus. However, Paul's testimony in Galatians suggests that his whole experience pushed him to do a lot of evaluations about himself, his teachings, and his work.

First, he had done some *theological reflections*. He claimed, "For I would have you know, brothers, that the gospel that was preached by me is not man's gospel. For I did not receive it from any man, nor was I taught it, but I received it through a revelation of Jesus Christ" (Gal 1:11–12). Paul was a zealous Jew who was willing to kill anyone who teaches anything inconsistent with the teachings of Judaism. His personal encounter with Jesus, however, challenged his core belief. After the encounter, he began to preach Jesus as the Christ/Son of God (Acts 9:20–22); this is something he would not have taught as a zealous Jew.

Second, he had done some *personal reflections*. He reminded the Galatians, "For you have heard of my former life in Judaism, how I persecuted the church of God violently and tried to destroy it. And I was advancing in Judaism beyond many of my own age among my people, so extremely zealous was I for the traditions of my fathers" (Gal 1:13–14). Previously, he considered it honorable to kill the followers of Jesus; now, he considered it contemptuous and realized that it was only by God's grace that he remained alive and became herald of the Gospel.

Third, he had done some *ministry reflections*. He further claimed, "he who had set me apart before I was born, and who called me by his grace, was pleased to reveal his Son to me, in order that I might preach him among the Gentiles" (1:15–16). During the early part of his ministry, he realized God's special assignment for him, and that is to preach to the Gentiles. Even though we can see his practice in Acts, how he made sure he first connected with the Jews by joining the synagogue meetings in every city he visited, he knew that his task was to be an apostle to the Gentiles.

Pastors need to be like hermits once in a while. The time we get away by ourselves could be a time for us to do theological, personal, and ministry reflections.

Sensitivity

Spiritual direction comes when we spent time with God. Luke recounts how Jesus choose the twelve apostles. He was able to choose his twelve apostles *after* he spent an extended period with God, "In these days he went out to the mountain to pray, and all night he continued in prayer to God. And when day came, he called his disciples and chose from them twelve, whom he named apostles" (Luke 6:12–13). This requires sensitivity to God's guidance.

While Jesus was with his disciples, he told them several times about his death. This suggests that he knew that the period of his earthly ministry would be short. However, God's work did not stop just because Jesus's earthly ministry was over. It should continue with the apostles. As Luke shows, Jesus did not haphazardly choose who to send out; he spent the whole night praying before choosing the Twelve. Luke's account suggests that the purpose of his overnight prayer was to seek spiritual direction from God as he chose the people who would continue his ministry. The church in Jerusalem also sought God's leading as they find a replacement for Judas (Acts 1:24–25), just as the church in Antioch was in prayer when they sent Barnabas and Paul as missionaries (13:2–3).

Choosing the right people for a work is not the only thing that requires God's guidance. The pastors must seek God's direction for their ministries. Paul's unplanned trip to Macedonia shows how important it is to constantly seek God's direction. Paul seems to have a systematic plan on how to preach the Gospel to the Gentiles. From Antioch, he first went to Galatia, the nearest region to the west. His plan was to continue westward and the next region in his list is Asia (Acts 16:6–10), which is also the closest region after Galatia. However, God had another plan. Paul was "forbidden" twice to go to Asia before he saw a vision of a Macedonian man calling, "Come over to Macedonia and help us" (16:9). He heeded and went to Philippi, then to Berea, Athens, and Corinth before going back to Asia where he originally planned. It seems that Paul's plan was perfect and strategic, one region at a time, from the nearest to the farthest, but it was not what God had planned.

These examples show that the pastors need God's guidance in all areas of ministry. Pastors must constantly seek God's direction for their work, whether they are doing their initial planning or mid course evaluation. Since the ministry is not really ours but God's, it is only right that we seek his plan on how he wants us to go about his work. Constant engagement with the Master clarifies our vision and concretizes our plans. Every minister of God must seek his guidance in order to do his will. Actually, God desires to have us more than he desires what we can do for him. This is what sets David apart from the other kings of Israel. He is known to be a man after God's heart (1 Sam 13:14; Acts 13:22). David G. Benner points out that the transformation of God's servants is of greater importance than the work that they can do for him.

> At the center of God's deepest desire for you is divine longing to complete your transformation. God's dream for you is that you become whole and holy as you find your identity and fulfillment in mystical union with the Lord God. Everything else is of

secondary importance—of significance only as it facilitates or impedes this journey.[6]

This does not undermine the importance of what we *do*. It simply means there is something more important than what we do, and that is what we become in relation to God. Growing in sensitivity to God's will requires we grow in love for him. Benner also explains,

> We become *discerning* about whatever it is that we love. Discernment is knowing the heart of our beloved. This is how our heart is aligned with the heart of our lover and our intimacy deepened. And this is exactly how it works with God.[7]

Discernment springs from our commitment to God himself, to grow in love for him, to become the person he wants us to be, and to do what he wants us to do. Discernment results from our belief that God is not only our Master who wants us to do his will, but he is also our heavenly Father who wants us to be conformed to the image of his Son.

THE PASTOR AS A HERMIT

Being a pastor can be overwhelming. The demands of the work itself can make the workers grow weary. Rest is the only solution for weariness. God has an open invitation to all of his ministers, "Be still, and know that I am God" (Ps 46:10a). Just as Jesus invites everyone, "Come to me, all who labor and are heavy laden, and I will give you rest" (Matt 11:28).

Pastors, like the rest of humanity, get tired and weary from their work. Hence, they need to be like hermits once in a while when they can have an extended time with God. An effective pastor RESTS in the Lord.

- Refresh: There must be a time for the pastor to recharge physically, emotionally, and spiritually.
- Examine: The pastors must learn to do self-examinations. They need time to ask God to search their hearts and reveal their innermost thoughts.
- Solitude: Time alone with God in solitude is a time well-spent.
- Think: The pastors need an extended time to think; to do theological reflections, personal reflections, and ministry reflections.

---

6. Benner, *Desiring God's Will*, 97.
7. Benner, *Desiring God's Will*, 98.

- Sensitivity: As pastors continue to do ministry, they must continue to develop both the keenness to know God's leading and the desire to be more like him.

Questions for Personal Reflection

Refresh: How do you make sure that you have a time to recharge and get ready for the next challenge in the ministry? How do you cope with physical exhaustion? with emotional exhaustion? with spiritual exhaustion?

Examine: How do you plan your schedule so that you can have a regular time to do self-examination? How do you make sure that even in self-examination, your focus is more on God and not on yourself?

Solitude: What is the greatest barrier or challenge for you to have a time of solitude with God? What practical steps can you do to overcome these barriers?

Think: What are some issues that you encountered recently that require you to do theological reflections? What are some personal matters you experienced that created a need for you to do personal reflections? What challenges or roadblocks related to the ministry that made you realize it is time to do ministry reflections?

Sensitivity: How can you continuously develop the sensitivity to God's leading? On a scale of 1–10 with 10 being the highest, how do you rate your love for God? What steps can you do to constantly improve in this area?

The Pastor is Not a Superhuman!

AFTER READING THE LAST twelve chapters, you may get the impression that to be a pastor, one must possess superhuman skills, flawless character, and tireless diligence. If you are a pastor or someone who is about to enter the pastoral ministry, before you get discouraged and quit, I suggest you first read the remainder of this chapter. Or if you are not a pastor, before you start evaluating your pastor or the pastors you know, I also suggest you first read the remainder of this chapter.

As we carefully consider the various roles of the pastors discussed in the earlier chapters, there are several important truths that we must bear in mind.

1. *The pastoral ministry has various expressions*
   Pastors may share the same calling, but they are gifted differently. They may serve the same God, but the same God gave them different passions and opportunities. They may share the same purpose, but their areas of assignment may be different. Thus, there can be many ways to do pastoral ministry, and here are some of its implications. First, we should not compare pastors with each other. The same Lord may assign pastors to various sections of his vineyard to do different work, but every pastor's work is important in view of the greater purpose of the one Master. Second, some pastors may focus on certain ministries more than the others. We cannot expect pastors to fulfill *all* the roles discussed above as this is impossible. Likewise, pastors must be careful not to think that pastors who focus on the other areas *are not* doing pastoral ministry. Third, it is wrong to assume that there is only one correct way of doing pastoral ministry. The needs of the congregation and community are determining factors how the ministry ought to be

done. The key is understanding *why* certain work is done, and with this understanding, the *how* and *what* can vary.

2. *The pastoral ministry requires both divine and human participation*

   The pastoral ministry requires diligence and effort on the part of the pastors, but they do not have to do the ministry by themselves. First, God did not design the ministry to be done only by the "professionals." Paul made clear that the pastor's task is to equip God's people so they can participate in his work. Getting people involved, removing unnecessary hindrances for people to serve while maintaining reasonable standards, creating opportunities, and providing help and training for the congregation are better than being a superhuman. Second, since the ministry is essentially God's work, it is God who will empower his workers to fulfill his work. The Scripture shows that it is through the Spirit of the LORD that God's servants, like Joshua, Gideon, David, Samuel, the prophets, John the Baptist, and Jesus, were able to fulfill the tasks assigned to them. This means that one does not have to be a superhuman to do pastoral ministry, but pastors definitely need to follow God's design of getting the right people involved and consistently depending upon God's empowerment in serving.

3. *The pastoral ministry is for those who are called, not for those who are perfect*

   The pastoral ministry is not for everyone. The Scripture teaches the priesthood of all believers, but it does not nullify the idea that certain people are called particularly to the role of elders. In the same way that the sons of Aaron and the Levites were called to a special task even if the nation of Israel was a kingdom of priests and a holy nation, there are individuals who are called to assume the pastoral role even if every believer is God's minister. The difference between the pastors and the believers in the congregation has to do with the roles and responsibilities they assume within the community of believers, and not their spirituality and Christian maturity. This does not mean we need not require certain level of maturity from those who enter the pastorate. It simply means that pastors, having the same kind of struggles like every member of the congregation, should also continue to aspire spiritual growth.

Bibliography

Adeney, Frances S. *Graceful Evangelism: Christian Witness in a Complex World*. Grand Rapids: Baker Academic, 2010.

Ball, R. Glenn, and Darell Puls. "Frequency of Narcissistic Personality Disorder in Pastors: A Preliminary Study." Paper presented to the American Association of Christian Counselors. Nashville, TN, 26 September 2015.

Barton Haley, Ruth. "It Begins with You! How the Spiritual Formation of Pastor Effects the Spiritual Formation of the Congregation." *CGJ* 7, no. 1 (2009) 26–36.

Bauer, Walter, Frederick W. Danker, W. F. Arndt, and F. W. Gingrich. *Greek-English Lexicon of the New Testament and Other Early Christian Literature*. 3rd ed. Chicago: University of Chicago Press, 2000.

Benner, David G. *Care of Souls: Revisioning Christian Nurture and Counsel*. Grand Rapids: Baker Books, 1998.

———. *Desiring God's Will: Aligning Our Hearts with the Heart of God*. Downers Grove: InterVarsity Press, 2015.

Bickers, Dennis W. *The Healthy Pastor: Easing the Pressures of Ministry*. Kansas City: Beacon Hill Press, 2010.

Blackburn, Bill. "Pastors Who Counsel." In *Christian Counseling Ethics: A Handbook for Therapists, Pastors & Counselors*, edited by Randolph K. Sanders, 75–85. Downers Grove: InterVarsity Press, 1997.

Blodgett, Barbara J. *Becoming the Pastor You Hope to Be: Four Practices for Improving Ministry*. Herndon: Alban, 2011.

Chapell, Bryan. *Christ-Centered Preaching: Redeeming the Expository Sermon*. Second Edition. Grand Rapids: Baker Academic, 2005.

Collins, Gary R. *Christian Counseling: A Comprehensive Guide*. Third Edition. Nashville: Thomas Nelson, 2007.

Confucius, Mencius, Zhuangzi, and Laozi. *The Four Chinese Classics: Tao Te Ching, Chuang Tzu, Analects, Mencius*. Translated by David Hinton. Berkeley: Counterpoint, 2013.

Dalton, Ron. *Discovering Christian Ministry: Theology and Practice*. Kansas: Nazarene Publishing House, 2015.

Dayringer, Richard. *The Heart of Pastoral Counseling: Healing Through Relationship*. Revised Edition. New York: Haworth Pastoral Press, 1998.

Dirks, Rudy. "A Pastor's Journey Toward Sabbath Rest." *Vision* 16, no. 1 (2015) 50–56.

Elmer, Duane. *Cross-Cultural Servanthood: Serving the World in Christlike Humility.* Downers Grove: InterVarsity, 2006.

Emlet, Michael R. "Loving Others as Saints, Sufferer, and Sinners (Part 2)." *JBCoun* 32, no. 2 (2018) 40–65.

Freeman, Donald A. "Five Important Characters of Ministry: Owned, Recognize, Empowered, Authorized, Accountable." *Prism* 16, no. 1 (2001) 53–60.

Greenway, Roger S. "Jesus, the Pastor-Evangelist." In *The Pastor-Evangelist*, edited by Roger S. Greenway, 1–14. Phillipsburg: Presbyterian and Reformed Publishing Company, 1987.

Hiestand, Gerald, and Todd Wilson. *The Pastor Theologian: Resurrecting an Ancient Vision.* Grand Rapids: Zondervan, 2015.

Hiltner, Seward. *The Counselor in Counseling: Case Notes in Pastoral Counseling.* New York: Abingdon-Cokesbury Press, 1950.

Homer, Paul L. "About Liturgy and Its Logic." *Worship* 50, no. 1 (1976) 18–28.

Hull, Bill. *The Disciple-Making Pastor: Leading Others on the Journey of Faith.* Revised Edition. Grand Rapids: Baker, 2007.

Köstenberger, Andreas J., and David W. Jones. *God, Marriage, and Family: Rebuilding the Biblical Foundation.* Second Edition. Wheaton: Crossway, 2010.

Leeman, Jonathan. "The Need for Pastoral Reasoning and the Recovery of Biblical Wisdom in Public Square Engagement." *CTR* 15, no. 2 (2018) 39–50.

Lewis, C. S. *The Screwtape Letters.* PTE Ltd., 1942. Reprint. New York: Harper Collins, 2001.

McMinn, Mark R., et al. "Care for Pastors: Learning from Clergy and Their Spouses." *PPsy* 53, no. 6 (2005) 563–81.

McNeal, Reggie. *A Work of Heart: Understanding How God Shapes Spiritual Leaders.* San Francisco: Jossey Bass, 2011.

Oden, Thomas C. *Classical Pastoral Care.* 4 vols. Grand Rapids: Baker, 1987.

Ogden, Greg. *Discipleship Essentials: A Guide to Building Your Life in Christ.* Expanded Edition. Downers Grove: InterVarsity Press, 2007.

———. *Transforming Discipleship.* Expanded Edition. Downers Grove: InterVarsity Press, 2016.

Oswald, Roy M., and Otto Kroeger. *Personality Type and Religious Leadership.* Lanham: Rowman and Littlefield, 2001.

Patrick, Dale, and James Kratz. "Making the Pastoral Prayer an Act of the Congregation." *Enc* 51, no. 2 (1990) 183–89.

Patton, John. *Pastor as Counselor: Wise Presence, Sacred Conversation.* Nashville: Abingdon, 2015.

Petersen, Bruce L. *Foundations of Pastoral Care.* Kansas: Beacon Hill Press, 2007.

Placher, William C. "Doubting Theology: Conversations that Count." *ChrCent* 121, no. 13 (2004) 25–36.

Prime, Derek J., and Alistair Begg. *On Being a Pastor: Understanding Our Calling and Work.* Chicago: Moody Press, 2004.

Purkiser, W. T. *The New Testament Image of the Ministry.* Kansas: Beacon Hill, 1969.

Richardson, Rick. *Reimagining Evangelism: Inviting Friends on a Spiritual Journey.* Downers Grove: InterVarsity Press, 2006.

Robinson, Haddon W. *Biblical Preaching: The Development and Delivery of Expository Messages.* Third Edition. Grand Rapids: Baker Academic, 2014.

Short, Peter. "Respect is the Beginning and the Way of Ministry." *Touch* 26, no. 2 (2008) 6–13.
Sisk, Ronald D. *The Competent Pastor: Skills and Knowledge for Serving Well.* Herndon: Rowman and Littlefield Publishers, 2005.
Stott, John R. W. *The Challenge of Preaching.* Updated by Greg Scharf. Cumbria: Langham Preaching Resources, 2013.
Vanhoozer, Kevin J. "Letter to an Aspiring Theologian." *FT* 285 (2018) 27–32.
Vanhoozer, Kevin J., and Owen Strachan. *The Pastor as Public Theologian: Reclaiming a Lost Vision.* Grand Rapids: Baker Academic, 2015.
Velander, Peter. "The Church Council is Driving Me Crazy!" *ClerJ* 78, no. 8 (2002) 3–6.
Wiest, Walter E., and Elwyn A. Smith. *Ethics in Ministry: A Guide for the Professional.* Minneapolis: Fortress Press, 1990.
Williams, Rowan. *Being Disciples: Essentials of the Christian Life.* Grand Rapids: Eerdmans, 2016.
Yount, Rick. "The Pastor as Teacher." In *The Teaching Ministry of the Church,* edited by William R. Yount, 45–73. Second Edition. Nashville: B & H Publishing, 2008.
Zylla, Phil C. "Inhabiting Compassion: A Pastoral Theological Paradigm." *HvTSt* 73, no. 4 (2017) 1–9.

Author Index

Adeney, Frances S., 84–85

Ball, R. Glenn, 17
Barton Haley, Ruth, 135–36
Begg, Alistair, 60–61, 66, 120
Benner, David G., 30, 139–40
Bickers, Dennis W., 110
Blackburn, Bill, 35
Blodgett, Barbara J., 32

Chapell, Bryan, 74–75
Collins, Gary R., 34, 38
Confucius, 6, 10

Dalton, Ron, 56–57
Dayringer, Richard, 30
Dirks, Rudy, 132–33

Elmer, Duane, 16, 21, 24
Emlet, Michael R., 6

Freeman, Donald A., 26

Greenway, Roger S., 77

Hiestand, Gerald, 88, 90–91
Hiltner, Seward, 37
Homer, Paul L., 123
Hull, Bill, 41, 44

Jones, David W., 118

Köstenberger, Andreas J., 118

Kratz, James, 127
Kroeger, Otto, 13

Leeman, Jonathan, 97
Lewis, C. S., 135

McMinn, Mark R., 115–16
McNeal, Reggie, 7

Oden, Thomas C., 29, 33, 122, 125, 131
Ogden, Greg, 46–49
Oswald, Roy M., 13

Patrick, Dale, 127
Patton, John, 25
Petersen, Bruce L., 30
Placher, William C., 97
Prime, Derek J., 60–61, 66, 120
Puls, Darell, 17
Purkiser, W. T., 99

Richardson, Rick, 81–82
Robinson, Haddon W., 72

Short, Peter, 22
Sisk, Ronald D., 7
Smith, Elwyn A., 4
Stott, John R. W., 71
Strachan, Owen, 65, 95

Vanhoozer, Kevin J., 65, 95
Velander, Peter, 13

Wiest, Walter E., 4
Williams, Rowan, 43
Wilson, Todd, 88, 90–91

Yount, Rick, 53

Zylla, Phil C., 30

Subject Index

accuracy, 66, 72–73, 75
administration/administrator. See manager.
admonition, 42, 45–47, 71, 90
adultery. See sexual practices.
affirmation, 54, 58–60
ambition, 18, 22, 26, 106
announcement, 6, 31–32, 46–48, 53–54, 65–66, 68–71, 77–82, 89–90, 96
apologist/apologetics, 2–4, 16–17, 49, 77–87
attitude, 2–3, 5, 9–12, 22–24, 68, 70, 73, 85, 108
authenticity, 30, 32–33

background, family. See upbringing.
baptism. See rites/rituals.
behavior/misbehavior, 9, 17, 46–47, 94
Bible. See Scripture.
blasphemy. See name (of God).
build up (Christ's body). See edification.

calling, 4, 56–57, 60, 81, 142
charisma, 11–12, 74
children. See family.
Commission, Great. See mission.
communion. See rites/rituals.
compassion, 5–6, 29–32, 57
consumerism. See covetousness.
contemplation, 94–95
convince. See persuasion.

covetousness, 50, 94
counselor, 2–3, 16–17, 25, 29–40
courtesy, 4, 8–9
culture, 1–2, 4–5, 7–10, 21, 23
customs, 8–10, 43, 128

deacons, 19–20, 60, 102, 107–108
delegation, 54–56, 60, 63, 100, 103–107
devotion, 33, 41, 49, 115
dialogue. See engagement (in theological conversation).
discipleship, 2–3, 16–17, 24–25, 32–33, 41–52, 61–62, 111
disciple-maker/disciple-making. See discipleship.
discipline, 6, 17, 49–50, 72, 115, 133, 135–36
disobedience. See persuasion.

edification, 2, 11, 13, 33, 38, 54, 56–59, 63, 66, 91, 123–24
education, 2, 8, 22, 59, 72
elders, 19, 23, 47, 60–61, 92, 99–100, 102, 107–108, 110, 113, 118, 126–27, 143
eloquence, 4, 22, 72–75, 78
empathy, 14, 17, 30, 35–37
empowerment, 17, 25–27, 55–56, 73, 143
encouragement, 16–17, 19–21, 29, 34–35, 50, 56–57, 62, 68–70, 127–28

SUBJECT INDEX

engagement (in theological conversation), 88–89, 96–97
envision. *See* vision.
equipping, 2–3, 13, 16–17, 24, 26, 34–36, 49, 51, 53–64, 77–78, 81, 85, 103, 117, 143
ethics/ethicists, 2–3, 17, 88–98
ethnicity, 4, 11, 21–22, 107
evangelist/evangelism, ix, 2–3, 14, 16–17, 20, 49, 57
examining (theological issues), 91–92, 94–95
examination, self, 133–35
exegete/exegesis. *See* interpretation.
exhortation, 66, 69–71, 75, 92, 120, 127–28
expectations, ix, 1–2, 23, 32, 61, 68, 110, 113–115, 117
explain/explanation, 42, 44–45

faith/faithfulness, 7, 11, 20–21, 23, 26, 32, 41, 45, 47, 53–63, 68–69, 73–74, 78, 81, 83, 89–92, 97, 100, 102–103, 112, 116–17, 124–25
family, 2–3, 5, 7–9, 16–17, 32, 37, 50, 54, 61, 69, 81–82, 91, 94, 96, 99, 102, 110–19

gifts, spiritual, 4, 11, 58–60, 102, 142
Golden Rule, 6, 59
good (practice), 114–15

healthy (practice), 116–17
hermeneutics. *See* interpretation *and* theology, contextual.
hermit, 2–3, 17, 131–41
homily. *See* preacher/preaching.
honor. *See* respect.
hope (for character transformation), 42, 47, 54, 61–62
hope, message of, 8, 71, 78, 80–81, 85, 95
humane, 5–6
human/humanity, 1–2, 4–15
humility, 3, 10–12, 22–24, 46, 70, 72–73, 96, 114–15, 122

idolatry, 50, 91, 94, 116, 132
imperative, divine, 112–14
insecurity, 26, 116
integrity, 23, 35, 41, 60, 72, 75
interpretation, 2–3, 16–17, 65–76, 95, 97, 123–24
introspection. *See* examination, self.

justice, 36–37, 50, 71, 89–90, 93–94, 117, 121–22, 133
kingdom of God, 18–19, 31–32, 50, 54, 67, 75, 78–80, 134
kneel. *See* prayer.
knowledge, 4, 57, 63, 72, 97, 137

labor, 78, 81–84, 88, 113
laity/lay people. *See* priesthood (of all believers).
Law, 7, 44–45, 50, 65, 67, 71, 75, 79–80, 96, 123, 128
lay ministry. *See* priesthood (of all believers).
leadership, 2–3, 7, 16–17, 19–20, 25–26, 30, 33, 35, 50, 54, 56, 60–61, 63, 73, 79, 82, 90, 93, 96, 100, 102–106, 113, 117, 120, 124, 126, 136
life, value of, 8, 12, 45, 50, 62, 71, 93–94, 132, 138
limitations, personal. *See* weaknesses.
listening, 31, 36–37, 41–44, 49, 67–70, 73, 75, 78, 89, 97, 113, 127, 136–37
liturgy/liturgist, 2–3, 16–17, 120–30

manager, ix, 1–3, 16–17, 99–109, 110, 112–15, 118
manners, 8–10
materialism. *See* covetousness.
mission, 7, 20, 23, 41, 48, 54, 57, 59–62, 77–78, 82, 85, 124, 139
motive, 2, 6, 17, 30, 45, 49, 55, 118, 133–34
murder. *See* life, value of.

name (of God), 34–35, 50, 72, 92, 94, 124
narcissism, 17–18

nature. *See* personality.
nurture, 29, 42, 49–50, 131

obedience. *See* righteousness.
offense, 8, 68–70, 84
order, household, 103, 114–15
order (of worship), 120, 122–24
oversee/overseers, 60, 99–103, 105–108, 110

parents. *See* family.
perfection/imperfection, 20, 32–33, 45–46, 48, 62, 118, 129, 143
perseverance (character), 12, 46, 62
perseverance (in preaching), 66, 68–70
personality, 2–3, 12–14, 22, 37, 74
personality-centered, 26, 74
persuasion, 2, 37, 67, 74, 78–80
plurality, religious, 50, 84–86, 94
prayer, ix, 20, 34–35, 42–43, 45, 50, 65–66, 73–75, 78, 82, 89, 93, 116–17, 121–24, 126–27, 133, 135–39
preacher/preaching, ix, xi, 16, 24, 30–31, 38, 48–49, 57, 65–75, 77–78, 80, 82–84, 90, 92, 96, 120–22, 124, 128–29, 134–35, 137–39
pride, 10–12, 16–17, 22–23, 26–27, 68, 85, 90, 122, 129, 134
priesthood (of all believers), 19, 26, 54–57, 60, 143
proclamation. *See* homily *and* announcement.
promotion. *See* ambition.
property, respecting other's, 50, 94, 121, 133
prophet/prophecy. *See* preacher/preaching.
propriety/impropriety, 5, 9, 50, 62, 103, 114–16

realistic, ix, 30, 33–35, 133
recruitment, 100–102, 106
redemption, 3, 6, 42, 65, 70, 75, 77, 89, 95, 111, 123, 125
referral, 35

reflect/reflection, 3–5, 16, 88–92, 97, 132, 137–38
refresh. *See* rest.
reproduction, 42, 47–49, 61
respect, 3, 5, 11, 18, 21–24, 45, 50, 58–59, 73, 85–86, 93, 113–14, 116, 118, 122, 125, 134–35, 137–38
responding (to people's needs), 7, 100, 106–108, 129
responsibility, 20, 24, 30, 32, 39, 46–47, 54, 56–59, 61, 65, 72, 85–86, 97, 100, 102–103, 105, 108, 110–12, 116, 120, 129, 143
rest, 3, 29, 45, 48, 50, 66, 70, 79, 94, 121, 123, 128, 131–33, 136
righteousness, 50, 95, 127
rites/rituals, 82, 120, 124–25

Sabbath. *See* rest.
sacrifice, 17–19
salvation. *See* redemption.
Scripture, 1–2, 4, 7–11, 16, 19–20, 22, 24–26, 29–30, 33, 38, 42, 44–45, 48, 60, 62, 66–68, 70–75, 77, 79–80, 83–85, 88–91, 93–95, 97, 99, 111, 113–14, 116–19, 126–29, 136–37, 143
self-righteousness, 9
selfishness, 6, 22, 26, 106, 135
sensitivity, 4, 8, 30, 37–39, 132, 138–40
sermon. *See* homily.
servant/servanthood, 2, 16–28
sexual practice, 9, 45, 50, 71, 94, 134
skills. *See* gifts, spiritual.
social concerns, 89–93
social skills, 4–5, 7, 9
solitude, 3, 132, 135–37
status, 2, 11, 18, 22
struggles. *See* weakness.

talents. *See* gifts, spiritual.
teacher/teaching, ix, 2–3, 9–11, 13–14, 16–17, 20, 23–24, 26, 31, 41–47, 49, 51, 53–64, 68–69, 72–73, 80–81, 84–85, 102–103, 114, 117, 122, 127–29, 138–143
teachers, false, 16, 47, 85, 96, 102, 132
team/teamwork, 19–21, 23, 60, 62

temptation, 32–33, 58, 62, 67, 71, 75, 80, 134
Testament, New. *See* Scripture.
Testament, Old. *See* Scripture.
testimony, 23, 33, 117–18, 122, 125, 134
thanksgiving. *See* prayer.
think. *See* reflect/reflection.
theology, contextual, 3, 16–17, 88–98
theology/theologian, ix, xi, 2–4, 11, 16–17, 22, 36, 72, 88–98, 129, 138
trainer/training. *See* equipping.
transformation, 2, 6, 8, 42, 45, 49, 135, 139

upbringing, 7–8, 35, 37

values, 1–2, 50, 57
virtues, 5–6, 11, 17, 23–25
vision, 2, 13, 47–48, 60–61, 100, 105–106, 139
vulnerability. *See* weakness.

weakness, ix, 6, 12–14, 20, 26, 30–33, 35–36, 41, 81, 102, 115, 118, 126, 143
witness, false. *See* justice.
worship, 3, 10, 16, 50, 74, 80, 83, 116, 120–24, 127, 129, 136

Scripture Index

Genesis

25:25	12
25:27	12
25:28	12
25:29–34	12
27:36	12
29:26	9

Exodus

2:11–12	8
12:37	54
18:13	54
18:18	54
18:19–20	54
18:21	56
18:21–22	54–55
20:1–22	50
20:3	94
20:4	94
20:7	94
20:8	94
20:12	94
20:13	94
20:14	94
20:15	94
20:16	94
20:17	94
20:22–26	50
20:26	10
21:1–11	50
21:12–32	50
22:1–15	50
22:22	93
22:26–27	6
23:1–9	50
23:10–12	94
28:4	10
35:5	58
35:21	58
35:22–24	58
35:25–26	58
35:34	58
36:1	59

Leviticus

11:15	132
12:3	7
20:9	50
20:10–21	50
20:11	50

Numbers

11:29	55
12:1–16	55
13:17–20	104
16:22–27	126
25:5	80
27:17	31
33:22	25
35:10	101

Deuteronomy

1:12–13	55

Deuteronomy (continued)

7:25	50
9:1	101
11:31	101
12:29–32	123
18:18	67
27:2	101

Joshua

1:5	100
1:7–8	101
1:8	43
1:11	104
3:5	101
24:15	113
24:31	113

Judges

2:7	113
7:1–18	103
17:6	113
21:25	113

1 Samuel

2:22–25	113
2:26	113
2:27–36	113
3:1–4	113
13:14	139

2 Samuel

6:20–23	116
22:28	11

1 Kings

7:14	58
8:22–61	136
11:1–3	116
12:4	80
12:9–11	80
12:14	80
16:31	116
16:29–17:1	132
18:1–19	132
18:20–40	132
19:1–3	132
19:4	132
19:5–7	132
19:8	133
19:9–18	133
19:19–21	133
21:1–16	133

2 Kings

13:23	6
22:17	31

1 Chronicles

22:15	58
25:7	58

2 Chronicles

2:7	58
2:13–14	58
10:4	80
10:9–11	80
10:14	80
18:16	31
26:15	58
30:22	58–59
34:12	58
36:15	6

Ezra

7:10	128
10:1	126

Nehemiah

1:2–3	105
1:5–7	106
1:8–9	106
1:10–11	106
2:1–8	106
2:9–17	106
2:12	105
2:12–14	106
2:17	106
2:18	106
2:18–20	106

2:20	106	79:8–11	37
3	106	94:4–6	37
3:1–32	106	101:5b	11
4:1–14	106	107:32	126
4:15–23	106	110:2	25
6:1–14	106	111	126
6:12	105	111:1	126
6:15–19	106	119:133	25
		137:1–4	36

Job

13:4b–5	37

		139:1–6	133
		139:23–24	133
		140:1–5	36
		142:3	37
		143:4	37
		149:1	126

Psalms

1:2	43		
4	43		
5	43	## Proverbs	
5:3	136	6:17	11
5:8–10	36	21:4	11–12
6:6	136		
6:6–7	36		
7:13–15	36	## Isaiah	
10:9	25	1:17	93
13:1–2	36	2:11	11
17:1–5	36	5:15	11
18:27	11	5:20	71
22:5–7	36	9:4	80
22:22	126	14:25	80
25:18	36	26:3	89
27:12	36	40:1	71
32:3–4	36	49:6	42
35:18	126	50	42
35:20	36	50:4	43–44
38:1–22	36	50:4–5	42
40:10	126	50:5	44
41:5–9	36	53	67
44:8–14	36	53:7	42
46:10a	140	59:8	89
49:11	25	61:1–2	66
55:2–7	36		
61:1–3	37	## Jeremiah	
64:1–5	36	3:14	25
68:26	126	6:13	90
69:1–5	37	6:14	89
73:1–28	37	8:11	89
74:1–3	37	17:9	135
74:2	126	22:3	93

Jeremiah (continued)

22:13	71
27:8	80
27:11–12	80
28:2	80
28:4	80
30:11	71
42:1–6	75

Ezekiel

2:6–7	69
9:9	93
13:10	90
22:3	71
37:11–14	71

Daniel

2:1–15	75
2:18	75
9:2	71
9:4–19	71
9:11	66
9:13	66
11:39	25

Hosea

12:7	93

Joel

2:28–32	67
3:3	93

Amos

8:4–6	93

Zechariah

7:9–10	93

Malachi

3:5	93
4:4	66

Matthew

3:2	80
4:8–10	80
4:1–11	33, 134
4:17	77, 80
4:23	77
4:25	44
5:10	50
5:17	44
5:21–22	45
5:27–28	45
5:31–32	45
5:33–34	45
5:38–39	45
5:43–44	45
5:48	45
6:1–2	50
6:1–8	45
6:5	50
6:5–8	127
6:6	136
6:7	136
6:16	50
6:16–18	45
7:22–23	17
8:1–9:34	31
8:4	45
8:20	18
9:31	82
9:36	31
9:37–38	32, 82
10:1–42	31
10:5–8	32, 53
10:7	48, 80
10:16–25	50
10:17–20	75
10:23–24	48
10:34	111
10:35–37	111
11:1	128
11:1–2	31
11:25–27	80
11:28	140
11:28–30	31
11:29	48
11:29–30	80
12:40	18

14:10–14	131	9:19	53
14:14	30	9:22	30
14:30	136	10:21	33
15:19	94	10:41	25
15:32	30	10:42	25
16:24–28	50	10:42–43	25
17:12	18	10:45	19
17:22	18	11:15–18	33
19:1	77	13:11	75
19:21	83–84	14:34–36	33
19:28	18	16:15–16	124
20:18	18	16:15–18	54
20:20	18		
20:20–28	25	**Luke**	
20:21	18	1:59	7
20:22	18	2:21	7
20:23	18	2:29–32	43
20:25	25	3:3	124
20:25–28	18	4:1–13	33, 134
20:28	18–19	4:16	128
21:12–13	33	4:17–21	66
22:15–16	86	4:18–19	70
22:23	86	4:21	66
22:34	86	4:43	82
22:37	137	6:5	18
23:2	128	6:12–13	138
23:12	24	6:35	9
26:39	33	7:13	30
27:43a	79	7:39	9
28:16	80	9:1–2	53
28:18–20	43	10:21	33
28:19	77	10:33	5
28:20	44	14:26	111
		17:17–18	9
Mark		18:9–14	10
1:4	124	19:10	18
1:15	80	19:45–48	33
1:35	43, 135	20:1	128
1:39	43	20:5–6	79
1:45a	82	20:45–47	93
3:14–15	48	20:47	93
5:34	89	21:1–4	93
8:31	18	21:4	93
8:32	30	22:19	125
9:9	18	22:24	19
9:12	18	22:25–27	19
9:14–29	53	22:26	19

Luke (continued)

22:26–27	20
22:31–32	20
22:32	20
22:33–34	20
22:39	43
22:42	33
24:27	67
24:44–47	67

John

1:36	81
1:41–42a	81
2:16	134
3:3	83
3:15	84
3:16	84
3:18	84
3:36	79
4:4	82
4:6	81
4:9	38, 107
4:10	84
4:13–14	39, 83–84
4:28–29	81
5:19	43
5:19–20	43
5:27	18
9:2–3	37
10:14	38
11:35	33
12:34	18
13:3–5	23
13:6–10	24
13:8	24
13:10–11	24
13:13–15	48
13:15	24
13:18–19	24
13:20	24
14:12	47, 48, 61
14:16–19	30
14:27	89
17:1–26	136
17:3	95
17:14–17	1
19:26–27	112

Acts

1:3	80
1:16	67
1:24–25	139
2:5–11	77
2:14–36	67
2:16–20	67
2:38	124
2:42	121
2:42–47	121
2:44–45	121
2:46	121
3:1–10	34
3:6	34
3:12–26	67
3:22–23	67
4:1–2	73
4:9	38
4:13–14	39
4:31	74
4:34	20
4:36–37	20
5:36–37	79
5:42	128
6:1	107
6:2–4	107
6:5	108
7:2–53	67
7:37	67
7:42	67
7:48	67
7:52	67
7:56	18
8:5	78
8:12	80
8:18–23	17, 134
8:25	77
8:26–39	78
8:30–35	67
8:30–36	85
8:35	42, 67
9:20–22	138
9:26–27	62
9:27	20
10:47–48	125
11:5–10	8
12:25	23

13	70
13–28	78
13:2–3	139
13:15	67, 70, 128
13:16	83
13:16–23	70
13:16–41	70, 83
13:17	83
13:18–19	83
13:22	83, 139
13:23–24	83
13:24–25	70
13:26–31	70
13:27	67
13:30	83
13:38	70
13:40	67
13:40–41	70
15	96
15:2	19
15:4	19
15:6	19, 92
15:13	92
15:16–41	67
15:21	128
15:22–23	19
15:35	128
15:36–40	62
15:38	20, 23, 62
15:39–40	62
15:39–41	20
16:3	96
16:4	19
16:6–10	139
16:9	139
16:25–26	121
16:27	121
16:32	121
16:30–34	121
17:2	67
17:2–5	73
17:3	95
17:4	79
17:11	73
17:13	73
17:22	83
17:22–32	83
17:26	83
17:28	83
17:29–31	83
17:32	83
18:4	78–79
18:13	78
18:24	72
18:26	72
19:8	78–80
19:16	25
19:26	78
20:7	121
20:25	80
20:28	100
20:29–31	47
21:15–17	29
22:16	124
24:16	134
26:28	79
28:23	67, 79–80
28:31	80

Romans

1:21	95
1:23	95
1:28–31	95
2:8	79
3:23	95
5:12–17	95
6:23	95
8:6–7	137
8:18–30	95
8:29	46
11:30	79
11:32	79
12:1	1, 123
12:1–2	121
12:2	137
12:3	11
12:10	22
13:7	22
15:14	46
15:26–28	121
16:17–18	26

1 Corinthians

1:11	36, 92

1 Corinthians (continued)

1:17	78
2:16	137
4:14	46
4:16	48
4:17	36
5:1–13	29
7:1	92
7:25	92
8:1	92
11:1	43, 48
11:20	125
11:23a	125
11:24–25	125
11:27	125
12:1	92
12:4–7	56
12:12–25	57
12:15–26	13
14:15	137
14:26	123
14:27–30	124
14:33	124
15:58	82
16:1	92
16:1–2	121
16:24	30

2 Corinthians

1:3–5	36
1:3–6	40
1:12	134
5:11	78
11:23	83
11:29–31	33

Galatians

1:11–12	138
1:13–14	138
1:15–16	138
1:17	137
2:2	96
2:2–3	96
2:3	96
2:5	96
6:1b	134

Ephesians

2:2	79
4:4–6	56
4:12–13	56, 58, 63
4:25–32	56
5:6	79
5:22–6:9	113
6:17	74

Philippians

1:15	134
1:22	82
2:3	22
2:6–11	92
2:16	82
2:19	36
3:5–6	7
4:9	89

Colossians

1:4	36
1:7–8	36
1:9	75
1:10	75
1:11	75
1:21	137
1:28	42, 47
3:6	79
3:16	46
3:18–4:1	113
4:3	74
4:7–9	36
4:7–14	62
4:14	62

1 Thessalonians

1:6	48
1:2–3	30
3:2	36
3:5	83
5:1	92
5:14	47

2 Thessalonians

2:1	92

SCRIPTURE INDEX

3:1	74
3:14–15	47

1 Timothy

1:5	134
1:3–4	47
1:15	91
1:19	134
2:1–4	126
3:1–7	23
3:2	22–23, 60, 102
3:3–4	23
3:4	23, 113, 115
3:4–5	99, 108, 110, 112
3:6	23
3:7	23, 60
3:9	60, 102
4:1	47
4:12	21
4:13	127
4:16	47
5:3–16	112
5:8	112
5:17	113
5:19–20	113
6:5	137
6:12	85

2 Timothy

1:4–7	61
1:6	69
1:7	69
1:8a	69
2:2	41, 47
2:11–13	92
2:15	73
3:2	9
4:10	62
4:11	21, 62
4:2	69, 78, 84
4:3–4	84
4:5	84

Titus

1:1–9	23
1:5	60, 101
1:6–9	102
1:9	60
1:10	47, 102
1:10–11	102
1:12	102
1:13	102
2:1–10	117
2:4–5	117
2:5	102
2:9	102
3:1	102

Philemon

23–25	62
24	62

Hebrews

1:1–2	70
2:1–4	70
4:6	79
4:11	79
4:12	74
4:14–16	32
5:7	33
9:11–28	70
10:12–18	70
10:19–25	29
12:16	12
12:28	9
13:17	79
13:22	70

James

1:4b	46
1:5a	46
5:14	126
5:16	127

1 Peter

2:13–3:7	113
3:2	22
3:1–7	116
3:7	117
3:15	85
5:1–3	20

1 Peter (continued)

5:1–5	29
5:2	100
5:3	25
5:5	24

Jude

3	85
16	85
18	85

Revelation

1:3	127

www.ingramcontent.com/pod-product-compliance
Lightning Source LLC
Chambersburg PA
CBHW071427160426
43195CB00013B/1835